TAKEN FOR GRANTED

TAKEN FOR GRANTED

How Conservatism Can Win Back the Americans That Liberalism Failed

—

GIANNO CALDWELL

CROWN
FORUM
NEW YORK

ISBN 978-0-593-13492-4

Ebook ISBN 978-0-593-13493-1

Printed in the United States of America

2 4 6 8 9 7 5 3 1

First Edition

Book design by Andrea Lau

CONTENTS

WHY I'M A BLACK CONSERVATIVE

"Yo, you gotta get your sister, man."

The stranger who'd stopped us was talking to my uncle, and the "sister" in question was my mom. It was morning. Springtime. I had been walking to school with my uncle, who was only five years older than me, when the man saw us and jogged across the street. I was nine.

"What do you mean?" my uncle asked. "What's going on?"

"She, you know . . ." The guy looked pained, considering his next words carefully, but eventually he pressed ahead. "She had sex with three or four dudes." He pointed. "Right inside that building."

She'd done it for drugs, I thought. He didn't have to say it. We all knew. Pills, marijuana, crack cocaine . . .

We stood together, an odd fellowship in this alley along 72nd Street, all of us looking at the vacant building. It loomed over us, a dead and empty thing with shattered windows and yellow skin peeling from the walls. Caught in its long shadow, I adjusted the book bag on my shoulder.

"Thanks," my uncle said. "Well . . . okay. Thanks."

I went to school, but the events of that morning festered all day. The embarrassment that, undeniably, the whole community knew. Multiplication tables and vocabulary quizzes now meant nothing to me. I could no longer pretend that our family was the only one who knew how bad it had gotten.

In high school, my mom had been an honor-roll student with perfect attendance, but in the years that followed, she had become an addict who'd do anything for more drugs. She now ran with the worst sorts of people. She sometimes left her own kids, including my two young sisters, alone with guys she'd just met while she snuck off to get high.

It's not like my family ever hid this fact, at least among ourselves. For us, *everything* was always out in the open. I grew up witnessing arguments and declarations of "We're poor!" or "You're high!" or "She's prostituting herself out to some drug dealer!" I grew up enduring this information, comfortable with the faint delusion that our family's problems were private.

But now I knew for sure. Our neighbors also knew what was going on. Some, it turns out, knew even more than I did. A year or so later, I would learn that my "uncle" was, in truth, my older brother. That my grandmother had adopted him and presented him to the world as hers when my mother got pregnant as a teenager.

After being stopped in the street that morning, things only got worse. Eventually, my grandmother demanded that my mother give over temporary custody of me and my siblings and go into rehab. "You gotta do it," she pleaded. *You gotta do it. You got to do it.* I remember going to the currency exchange at 75th Street and Stony Island, next door to Jackson Park Hospital, and watching my mom get the paperwork notarized. "I give custody of my children . . ."

For the first time in memory, I felt a bit of relief. This was a new chance for all of us. A chance that my mom would get the help she needed and things would be okay again. That my siblings and I would move to a safer environment, one farther away from the epicenter of the gangs and violence, where we wouldn't have to rely on government housing. A chance that we'd have somebody who'd actually look after us. That I had a future beyond my present.

But real change doesn't come easy. And that road to a better future would be tougher to walk than I could ever imagine.

MAYBE YOU DON'T KNOW the South Side of Chicago. Maybe you know a little, that it can be rough and heartbreaking and oftentimes deadly.

I grew up in a house of addiction, poverty, government assistance, divorce, neglect, abandonment, and violence. This wasn't a unique experience in my neighborhood, or in neighborhoods like it across the United States. A lot of kids had mothers or friends or family on drugs. People willing to do anything to get more. Many had brothers in gangs or in jail. Sisters addled on crack. Fathers and boyfriends who vanished—or, worse, stuck around with only their fists.

There was a club at my school, and everyone knew who its members were. There was no hiding it. From the stink of your unwashed clothes to kids cracking "jokes" in the lunchroom about your mom or dad being an addict or worse. Some kids came to school with fresh bruises every week.

If you were in this club, other students would rip on you. This was to be expected, I suppose. But the teachers also looked at you differently. Not with empathy or even pity. More like, they looked *through* you. As if your future was already written on your dirty clothes, in your weary eyes, on your dark skin.

Of course, "inner-city" Chicago could also be quite beautiful. The sound of genuine laughter from front porches and street corners as people told stories or played the dozens—a game in which two people square off in a friendly verbal war of insults. The sound of a choir on Sunday in a church that only held fifty. Kids playing basketball. Playing tag with friends, dashing past an open fire hydrant in July. Riding my bike all day past stores and getting ice cream from the ice cream truck on the rare days we could afford it.

I have genuine love for my hometown and roots. And, despite the hardships we faced, I grew up in a home of faith and hard work and prideful self-reliance.

But it's also true that the bike from my memories was eventually stolen from me. A gang member plucked me off, set me aside, and pedaled off without a single word. I never saw that dude, or the bike, again. It's almost funny now. Almost.

Even as an adult, at times, when I passed through the South Side or visited it as part of some news story I was shooting, my whole chest would still clench. My stomach sometimes roiled and turned. It was the same genuine panic I felt as a kid whenever I'd come back to the South Side after staying with my father or grandparents in a better neighborhood. Every time, *every* time, I was brought back to be with my mom, I was filled with palpable dread. Within inner-city Chicago, I could *still* fear the same danger and depression as before. Amplified by the fact that I'd gotten out, even more aware. Sure, I can play it off well if I'm on camera. That's the job. But there's an echo from what I felt as a child.

I remember when I first managed to move out into an apartment of my own. Even then, my childhood was never more than a few blocks away. The empty lots, the people torn down and hopeless. And always knowing that this is where I came from. Yes, I felt great compassion for those still living in those circumstances. But the anxiety remained, maybe even grew during those days, because I never wanted to live like that again.

Today, I appear regularly on the most-watched news channel on earth. I run a successful consulting firm that makes good money and also makes the world a better place. I've got apartments in L.A. and D.C. People say I've "come far."

I suppose there's truth to that. But I wrote this book to focus on an overlooked part of my perceived accomplishments. If I've achieved beyond any statistical or cultural expectations, if I've managed to play the cards dealt with some manner of success, it's because:

1. I've relied on a core set of "conservative" values to make it happen.

2. I was not alone on this journey.

And the best thing is, I'm just getting started.

OH, HE'S A *CONSERVATIVE*?

Well, it's in the subtitle of this book. And yes, I eventually figured out that's exactly where my values lie. That I:

Praise God and support Judeo-Christian values.

Respect and believe in the promise of the American Dream.

Trust the free market and the spirit of the entrepreneur.

Reject the size, scope, and intrusion of government in our lives.

Believe in individual liberty and personal responsibility.

Know that a democratic republic can produce and defend laws that secure equality and social justice for all.

Beyond what these conservative values have done for me personally—which is everything—I've also seen these same ideals change other people's lives and the conditions of communities at the local, state, and federal level. I've seen them work for people across the country, people of all life experiences and challenges.

Will half the country not even pick up this book because I'm a conservative? Am I only preaching to the choir? I certainly hope not. If I used the term "traditional" or "small-town" values, would that help? (Then again, "small-town" wouldn't be right. Three million people live in Chicago.)

I've heard all the labels.

The "black Republican."

The "traditionalist millennial."

The "Uncle Tom."

The "Never Trumper." The "*Always* Trumper."

The "talking head" on TV.

Forget the labels. I did. Long ago. Here's what I know instead.

My core principles, more than anything else, are what saved

me from becoming a statistic. The same conservative values that have saved hundreds of millions of people—whether they know it or not—and still draw people from around the world to the United States every day.

In our current political landscape, too many Americans are taken for granted.

From those living in the inner city to the factory workers and owners of small businesses in the one-stoplight towns throughout our country. Liberalism and the Democratic Party have all too often held up the "American Dream" as something to mock and distrust. It's a myth, they claim. A lie to keep those with power and riches safely entrenched where they are. All of those *millions* who'd arrived as immigrants (or clawed their way out of government housing) decade after decade to join the middle class or far beyond, sending their own kids off to college, building billion-dollar companies—those were just "anecdotal" tales to perpetuate the lie.

Upward social mobility could not be achieved, the liberals argued, *without* government assistance; and equal opportunities for prosperity required more regulation, not less. Meanwhile, those most trapped within the system built by these ideals were slipping further and further away from prosperity.

I'm writing this book because I believe the American Dream isn't a fairy tale—or, worse, some liberal punchline. I believe these values can propel this country, me, *and* you to the heights we were always meant to reach.

And I believe it, most of all, because that's how it happened for me.

WHEN I WAS EIGHTEEN, I wanted to own property.

I'd been inspired by my pastor, Dr. Bill Winston, who'd been pushing members of the church to go out and own something— real estate, a business, stocks—and by the guest speaker he'd brought in to emphasize that message: Farrah Gray.

Gray was a young black businessman and motivational speaker from Chicago. He grew up in the projects, but by the time he was six years old, he had started a business making homemade lotions and painted rocks. Through various endeavors in everything from prepaid phone cards to a food company targeted at teens, he'd become a millionaire by age fourteen. This guy had persevered through the most abysmal of circumstances, making his way out of some of the same projects I'd lived in as a kid and creating wealth for himself and his family. I was inspired by his testimony and his ability to ignore the naysayers along the way.

Less than one year later, I purchased a multiunit apartment building for myself. This happened without any assistance from friends or family. Had they known what I was up to while I was in the process, they probably would have discouraged me. They'd never done anything like that themselves, and nobody around me believed I would be any different. The only people in my family I told about my plans were my Aunt Patricia and my godmother, Barbara, neither of whom ever questioned my "wild" dreams and ideas.

My grandmother, who largely raised me and my siblings, often told me that my older brother was going to be the successful one and I was not. I'll never know if this was because she'd raised my older brother as her own son or because out of the nine siblings in my family (by seven different fathers), I was the only one with an *active* father, and this was her way of evening the playing field. Today, she only tells me that she was wrong. But the greater tragedy, far beyond any pain I felt at her early assessment, is that my older brother has been in and out of jail for years. These days, I feel more saddened than angry when I think back on her bleak outlook. But I share my grandmother's words here to show that this was the bar that had been set for me.

To her, and others, my future was already cast.

The poverty made it so. My parents.

My schooling. My block.

The color of my skin.

This is why I feel for individuals who find themselves surrounded by loved ones who don't think they can do better than those who came before them. Environment plays such an important role in determining your mindset and motivation. In a lot of cases, the concept of what you can be is based on the people around you and what they give you.

This isn't an issue relegated to any one neighborhood, creed, or tax bracket. Recently, I was in the Fox News makeup room with a successful, white, hyper-educated producer and her sixteen-year-old daughter. We began to chat. "What are your plans for college?" I asked the teen.

"I wanted to go to Brown . . ." she said excitedly, before looking down. "But I'm not going to apply because I won't get in."

"Why would you say that?" I asked, genuinely surprised.

"Because my guidance counselor told me to be realistic," she said.

Behind her, her mother nodded in agreement.

I was beyond disappointed. This girl was barely sixteen. "Be realistic" is not only unhelpful advice, it is harmful. It is a dream killer.

We have to let go of the fallacy that so many people buy into: "My dad was a truck driver, so I have to become one, too." "No one in my family ever went to college, so I probably won't either." "I can't get into a school like Brown." "Moving to New York or Paris or Singapore to pursue a career in X is a one-in-a-million chance, so . . ."

My own grandfather, a hardworking plumber and small business owner, had his own ideas about my future. He thought I would continue the family business. He was the first to have faith in me, in my abilities, before anyone else in my family, yet that was the full extent of the life he'd imagined for me.

But that did not stop me from pursuing careers in government, lobbying, consulting, and television.

Such possibilities will likely not "reveal" themselves as some cookie-cutter path that you or I can just walk down with ease. We have to *create* such paths ourselves, with determination and the knowledge that God is right up there creating for us. That's why I always tell people to aim as high as they can. Don't look at Oprah Winfrey or Barack Obama or Steve Jobs or anyone who's achieved great success and think, *They're just exceptional.* They are *not* exceptional. They just refused to succumb to limiting beliefs and found a way to tap into their full potential.

I rose out of poverty and reached professional heights that few people thought possible—including myself—but I, too, am not exceptional or special. I'm certainly not the first kid to make it out of the projects, nor am I the first black conservative you ever saw on TV. I am not the first person on earth to achieve more than was expected of him. Many, in fact, work to overcome even greater obstructions of health or upbringing or financial ruin than me. My desire is not to compete with those who've had it worse or better, but only to expose the terrible lie of limitations and share the values that made the next steps possible for me.

All of us have been constrained in one way or another. Limited by societal expectations. By our own families. By words. Limited by where we get our ideas, and whom we'll work with to solve the big problems and achieve grand dreams. Limited by our own self-doubt. But when I first started following fundamental conservative values, it ended all of that for me. It destroyed all such limitations by giving me faith in God, faith in the process, and, ultimately, faith in myself.

It's why I walked into an alderman's office at age fourteen to get my first internship. It's why I started working part-time for the federal government by sixteen. It's why I figured out how to earn a college degree. Why I started my own consulting firm in Washington, D.C. Why I became a political analyst, correspondent, and host on television. Why I moved to Los Angeles, where I could pursue those things and others to a greater degree.

The term "crab mentality" comes from the phenomenon that occurs when one crab attempts to escape a bucketful of crabs and the others work together to pull the hopeful escapee back into the bucket. Remind you of anyone you know? Each of us is shaped in an environment that can, if we let it, contain and constrain our truest self and potential.

Look around, though, and you'll spot people everywhere who've transcended that influence. They come in all shapes and colors and industries. Technology, social justice, music, sports, politics. These are the ones who've rejected the limitations of dependency and victimhood and expectations of humanity at its lowest.

This book is my attempt to share with you the times I've had to break down such walls and to challenge whatever the status quo might be. Each time I've done so, it has been with the strength and confidence I've discovered as a conservative.

My journey has not come without the loss of friends and family, without missteps and retreats. And my journey is not yet over.

But I've lived the other life—the one many find themselves trapped in every day—a life painted by the fears and expectations of others. Community, family, friends. They say: *You are this race, gender, age, zip code, education,* and so on. *Therefore,* this *is the future you will have.* It is the safe way, the known way. The way that is perceived to have worked before. It is the way you, your greatest detractor, often see for yourself.

Forget that way.

In matters of politics, faith, career, relationships, and self-growth.

I am a conservative for two reasons.

First, these values work. They've worked for generations before me and for me personally.

And second, I had no other choice.

The alternative—a life of self-doubt and dependence and victimization—was a path that led only to some decrepit building on 72nd Street.

Whether for me personally or for the United States as a country, I knew the better course lay in finding truth and strength in a set of values that were here long before me and would continue long after. I would no longer be taken for granted.

My hope is that in discussing these values in terms of today's issues, politics, and my own life, I may convey to others that conservatism isn't some "bitter old man's" attempt to keep things as they once were in the past. Instead, it is a powerful beacon, a verified force . . .

. . . for how things should be in our future.

TAKEN FOR GRANTED

1

A SPY FOR OBAMA

MY INTRODUCTION TO THE GOP

NOT LONG AGO, I walked up to a well-known black actress to introduce myself, someone you'd know from the movies she's starred in. As I extended my hand, she shot back a damning look of revulsion. "I know who you are," she said. "You're that Republican from Fox News." It was the end of *that* conversation.

Another time, at a Hollywood party, I was having a great chat with another popular actress and comedian. Just as we were about to exchange contact information, it became clear I was a Republican, and the conversation ended abruptly, without another word, as she turned and walked away. I stood there alone for a long time, like a kid stuck against the wall at an eighth-grade dance.

A couple years ago, on a blind date, the two of us got around to discussing our work. "Oh my God!" my new friend gasped, as if she'd just discovered she was sitting in the car with Jack the Ripper. "You work for Fox News ... and you're ... a ...

Republican." She asked the Uber driver to stop the car—you can't make this stuff up—and was going to walk away, at night, in the middle of nowhere. We ultimately agreed to have the driver drop her off safely at home.

Most times, when someone learns I'm a Republican, the reaction is one of dismay or disgust. White folk usually fall within the dismay category ("I assumed you . . ."), while members of the black community, as shown in all three of these examples, often look at me as the worst kind of enemy. A traitor. A . . . you got it, "Uncle Tom."

Can I blame any of them? The truth is, I don't. More than a decade ago, I thought similarly.

If you asked what party I belonged to then, I'd have told you I was a Democrat. This had little or nothing to do with my actual beliefs. Rather, I knew this because everyone around me—family, neighbors, friends—was a Democrat, and more than 70 percent of voters keep the same political allegiances as their parents. I knew this because I was black, and almost 90 percent of African American voters identify with the Democratic Party.

I also knew all about the Republicans. All the "facts."

The ones ingrained in me and many members of the black community since birth. "Republicans are racist." "They don't care about black people, don't care about poor people." "They want black men in jail—or, better, dead from drugs or gang violence." "Republicans are the party of racist, rich white people." "Republicans created and led the KKK." "They try to keep blacks from voting." "The GOP intentionally blocks the advancement of blacks and always has." "If you ever become one, you'll get kicked out of the family and be an 'Uncle Tom' and a 'coon.'"

Maybe you find these accusations and words offensive. I certainly do. Maybe you agree with some of them and think they're worth debating. All I'm telling you is that this was the narrative as I knew it. At the time, *everyone* I knew thought exactly the same way. During the formative years of my life, I had no clue what a Republican—or a conservative—even was. As a result, I had no idea who *I* was politically.

GROWING UP on the South Side of Chicago, I heard it all the time. From my parents and friends, my teachers, my girlfriend and her grandmother, the guy working next to me. It was always the same spin on things: The Republicans were the "racist party" who spent their days keeping people of color down.

The message even held sway in our churches. For decades, Democratic politicians have gone to pastors in black communities and given them their talking points and marching orders. These pastors see that the Democrats have something they need—sources of income, ways to expand their reach, influence with the mayor—and the next thing you know, some politician is standing in the middle of a service giving a partisan speech. Chicago's ex-mayor and former Obama chief of staff Rahm Emanuel was infamous for popping into black churches, giving a quick talk, and walking out before the next hymn even started. (How often do you see a black politician speaking in a white church, or *any* politician taking over a Catholic mass or synagogue service to give a speech? You don't.) That's how entrenched the Democrats' agenda, and falsehoods, were in my community.

So why would I think differently? My family, my friends, my school, and even my pastors at the time were all saying the same things. Where would such differing ideas even come from? More troubling, who would support those ideas if I dared have them?

It wasn't worth the time to investigate the matter further. The earth was round, wood floats, and the GOP was basically the KKK in better-looking jackets. And "better-looking" was debatable.

Then, one evening, as I was talking on the street with a neighbor I hardly knew, there was a catalyst—or at least the chance for one—that helped change my narrative. I was barely twenty. We were discussing politics, each of us pontificating on this and that, when this older black gentleman openly challenged me on one of my viewpoints.

I don't remember the specifics of what I'd said, but it had been something nasty about the GOP and some social injustice I'd laid at their feet. Whatever criticism I'd just made, this man didn't simply let it pass or look the other way when such inaccurate "facts" were being shared. He knew my take was wrong, and he did what few ever do in a closed community: He pushed back. "Where'd you get that?" he said. "That's not right."

He mentioned that most black people had once been Republicans themselves. I'd never heard that before, so I didn't believe it. Out of pure shock that this guy would openly lie to me like that, my tone became more aggressive.

The gentleman held out his hands. "Listen," he said. "I'm not trying to convert you. *I'm* a Democrat. But what you're saying is . . . wrong."

Whatever defense or counterargument I may have tried that night, it didn't hold up for long. Clearly this man knew more than I did, so I stopped talking and told myself that he and I would meet again.

Here's something you should know about me. Whenever I'm

challenged, I always go off to find more information, in hopes that I'll have a stronger argument in the conversations to come. I hoard facts like a magpie preparing for his next debate.

In the eighth grade, for example, if I knew that our teacher, Mr. Horton, was going to discuss a particular subject, I would always research ahead in order to debate him. I wanted to stand out in class. I was the kid who'd scour the dictionary for a word I'd never heard anyone use, just to see if Mr. Horton knew it. Although it was his first year teaching, he always knew the word, and he stayed one step ahead of me in all of our arguments. (Still, this strategy endeared me to Mr. Horton, who believed I had a real future in politics. When I ran for class president and it didn't look like I was going to win, he informed the class that he'd likely use his weighted vote for a Caldwell presidency, swaying more voters my way.)

At some point, I knew, there would be a round two with the man who'd challenged my opinion out on the street. If I wanted to fare better next time, I had work to do. So, for the first time in my life, I researched the legislative and philosophical distinctions between the GOP and the Democrats. I got on the Internet and typed in *difference between Republicans and Democrats.*

The search engine filled with thousands of results, and then tens of thousands. I started reading. Minutes became hours as my eyes raced through the websites. More than once, I looked over my shoulder, worried that a friend would come in and catch me reading about Ronald Reagan.

I couldn't believe what I was reading—in particular, the supposed history of the two parties. These websites claimed that the Republicans first formed to *stop* the spread of slavery to the west (*free soil, free speech, free labor, and free men*) and then, under President Abraham Lincoln, worked to end slavery altogether. It was the *Republicans,* too, who crafted and then led the way to the Thirteenth Amendment (which abolished slavery), the Fourteenth Amendment (which granted citizenship to blacks), and the Fifteenth Amendment (which gave black men the vote). Every major civil rights bill from Lincoln to Martin Luther King, Jr., was driven by and supported by the GOP.

It was all BS, of course. Republican propaganda. More "white lies."

It had to be. *Right?*

Besides, these websites *looked* like propaganda, with their unprofessional designs and walls of featureless text. (I'm reminded of the U.S. Supreme Court case *Jacobellis v. Ohio* and Justice Potter Stewart's "I know it when I see it" line.) No matter how many sites I found that gave the same info, I didn't believe it. I sat there baffled. *Who went to all the trouble to create these propaganda websites?* That was the biggest mystery to me. I had to know more.

BEFORE I GO ON, let me stress that this chapter is not about how the Republicans are the greatest party ever, and how this unimpeachable truth was hidden from me all my life. The GOP, as it exists today, is not perfect. However, it's the party with which *my* conservative beliefs are most aligned and where I feel my voice has the greatest impact.

Your best match may be with another party. That realization and decision could come in your teens or much later. Hillary Clinton and Elizabeth Warren both began as Republicans. Warren, for her part, switched worldviews in her late forties. Ronald Reagan was a Democrat until his early fifties.

This could very well cause some friction with your parents, spouse, friends, co-workers, and others. Political shifts *have* cost marriages and jobs. The entertainment and IT industries are notoriously liberal, and conservatives risk a lot if they speak up in the presence of their colleagues there. Or imagine being a Bernie Sanders supporter while working in the upper echelons of the Pentagon, or growing up in Lubbock, Texas (statistically speaking, the most conservative town in America). Or being the one with the Make America Great Again hat at your family's Rosh Hashanah dinner. (For the past fifty years, Jewish American voters have been almost as loyal to the Democrats as African Americans.)

My desire in writing this chapter is only that more people will do the digging necessary to make such choices freely, and then have the courage to stand up to the pushback that most likely will come. To not just pick the party of their parents, classmates, neighborhood, or industry. To not just pick a party because they've swallowed fifty years of misinformation. To not be intimidated into groupthink.

Because, for twenty years, that's what I did.

Any semblance of *real* choice had been hidden from me.

I WAS NOT NEW to discussions of politics or government. And my path to these heated street-corner debates wasn't just academic. It was personal. It began when I was fourteen.

One morning, just after daybreak, my grandfather—the one who owned the plumbing business—was driving us through Englewood, a neighborhood on the South Side of Chicago. Almost every Saturday, he'd take me along with him as he visited his job sites around town. He drove a red truck with the back filled with plumbing supplies and the words "Master Card and Visa Accepted" painted on the doors. On these site visits, he would check on the work being done and sometimes let me help when I could.

Englewood was one of the roughest neighborhoods in Chicago, riddled with gangs, violence, drugs, and prostitution. Worse, that day was already hot and sticky even before 8 A.M. The sooner we moved on to the next location, the better.

Then, looking out my rolled-down window, I saw her.

My mother. *Had to be her.* Walking down the street. Same size, dressed in the same clothes. She looked beat down and drugged up. I hadn't seen her in almost a year. Lately she was always going off on drug binges and losing touch with us. I knew this was a part of town she'd come to, but I never liked to think of it much. Now I had no choice but to see it with my own two eyes.

Tears started to well up in those two eyes as my whole body tensed.

"What's wrong with you, boy?" he asked in his deep southern drawl.

"Nothing," I mumbled, struck to my core with hot, sickening embarrassment. My grandfather had followed my gaze. He, too, did a double take, reading my mind. It hadn't, I realized, been my mother. But my grandfather and I both knew it *could* have been.

We continued to ride in silence. I kept my head turned so my grandfather wouldn't see my tears. But through the sadness and pain of memory and disappointment, thoughts began to race through my head. *I wish things were different. How can I make them different? What can I do?*

When enough blocks had passed and we were well and truly gone, I angrily brushed the tears away—tears that had never helped anyway, no matter how much I'd begged my mother to change—and turned to my grandfather. "How . . . how do we get her . . . how can people get the help they need?" I asked quietly. "How can we punish the drug dealers more?"

My grandfather did something I never expected. He didn't rant or rave. He didn't blame anybody, really. He simply began to talk about elected officials—the influence they wield and their power to make change.

His words gripped me with a powerful urgency, a sense of rightness as true and real as anything I'd ever experienced in my life. I wanted that power to effect change. I needed it. At that moment, at the ripe old age of fourteen, I decided I was going to become an elected official.

The very next week, I visited my local alderman's office to sign up as a volunteer and learn the political process. Before long, I became an intern, and that internship led to another internship, at the largest county treasurer's office in the state of Illinois. After that, when I was sixteen, I started a part-time job with the federal government for the Social Security Administration. After graduating high school, I worked there full-time in various roles.

This is where I was working when I got pulled into that street-corner discussion of Republicans and the uncomfortable realization of my own limitations regarding history and truth.

All that summer, I kept digging, and kept finding the same thing.

It was southern *Democrats* who'd used Jim Crow laws to segregate and marginalize black people. *Democrats* who'd put fire hoses and dogs on my ancestors; who'd used welfare and poverty to guarantee the black vote for fifty years, creating a cycle of victimization that's lasted generations.

All of these crimes that had been presented to me as creations of the Republican Party . . . weren't. In the same thread, it was the GOP, not President Lyndon Johnson, that had pushed through the Civil Rights Act of 1964. Johnson was more, "These Negroes, they're getting uppity these days. We've got to give them a little something. Just enough to quiet them down, but not enough to make a difference." And how about "civil rights leader" John F. Kennedy? Turns out he voted *against* the Civil Rights Act of 1957 while he was a senator, *opposed* the 1963 March on Washington, and wiretapped and investigated Dr. Martin Luther King via the FBI.

Speaking of Dr. King, he was once a Republican. And it was Republican Richard Nixon who supported and enforced the *first* affirmative action; Republican Dwight Eisenhower who sent federal troops into Arkansas to desegregate Little Rock Central High School; Republican Ronald Reagan who made King's birthday a national holiday and filed more civil rights suits in housing, education, and voter discrimination than his predecessor, Democrat Jimmy Carter. The same trend was true at the state level. Hiram Rhodes Revels of Mississippi, a Republican, was the first black ever elected as a U.S. senator. Republican Joseph Rainey of South Carolina was the first black to enter the House of Representatives. (In fact, the next *twenty* African Americans in the House would all be Republicans.) Pinckney Pinchback of Louisiana—a Republican—was the first black governor of a U.S. state. Well into the 1950s, white Republicans were called "Black Republicans," a slur meant to shame them for supporting African Americans too vigorously.

I was finding this information in too many places. And this

history resonated with me, caring as I did about empowering my community. There must be *some* truth to this. To explore further, I went back to my friends and family, people I looked up to, and asked if *they* knew anything about this. My family said they'd never heard any of this before and told me not to get sucked into the Internet's lies. They *all* said it was propaganda. No one believed it. I felt like Galileo proposing a new theory about how the universe works. In my little corner of the world—which at that point was my *entire* world—I had committed the sin of heresy. But, for me, the major premise of that world ("The GOP is the historically racist party") had been shattered. Now all the political arguments that followed also were questionable. I had to learn more. So I kept reading.

The GOP, I discovered, was a religious, pro-Christian party. It held "conservative" values and views regarding faith, family, and culture. It championed self-reliance and hard work. It believed that capitalism and the free market had quickly created the largest middle class in the history of civilization. It believed in individual freedoms and God-given rights over mob rule and intrusive government. It believed in the sanctity of law.

Just like me. Just like, according to polls, half of *all* African Americans.

My grandfather, a small business owner, often griped about overtaxation and overregulation. He said these policies would drive him out of business. He sometimes talked about how some of his biggest deals had dried up after competitors started using illegal immigrants to slash bids and undercut him. Republicans—as if hearing my grandfather's specific concerns—also wanted lower taxes, fewer regulations, and better control over the immigration process to make sure all employers were playing by the same rules.

I was rattled. These GOP policies felt like a reflection of . . . me. My beliefs. I was trying to deal with the ramifications of this realization. How could I possibly see this system that was so racist—based on *everything* I'd ever been told—as a reflection of myself? *This can't be real!*

My confusion soon turned to anger.

Anger at others. And at myself.

How had I been so easily bamboozled? So misinformed? So lied to?

My family, all these people, the black community . . . they were both perpetrators and victims. They believed and spread the narrative that Jim Crow segregation was a Republican thing, and that rich white men were the lone and total group Republicans actually cared about. I, along with everyone else I knew, had been robbed of the right to find out what we *truly* believed. I had been denied that opportunity by my own family, neighbors, friends, teachers, and even pastors.

What's more, we had been encouraged to act in a particular way because of these lies, offering Democrats our votes and support.

The Democrats had effectively influenced the black community for decades using this narrative. And they still are.

Hakeem Jeffries (D-N.Y.), the chairman of the House Democratic Caucus, called President Donald Trump "the Grand Wizard of 1600 Pennsylvania Avenue." And Joe Biden warned: "They just want to put you back in chains." (Imagine the outcry if a Republican had said this!) Both were emotional statements, with little reference to rational thought or reality. But if you're African American, it still connects with you. *How can it not?* Yes, slavery ended 150 years ago, but the consequences of it, and the racism connected to it, have not. Mention of slavery or segregation or racism still evokes deep and profound emotions in the black community, and it probably always will.

People in general are swayed by emotion. How much of Trump's improbable victory in 2016, for example, was driven by America's emotions? But in the black community, this is particularly true. You can't control us with our money, because there's not enough wealth in the black community for that to matter. You can't talk about tax policy, because there aren't enough people who will benefit from that. The same goes for today's other hot-button issues. LGBT rights? Immigration? *Are you serious?* African Americans are still largely fighting for our own rights.

And so, instead of discussing these other issues, liberal politicians usually produce an emotional argument or statement that leads back to slavery, Jim Crow, or racism. The Democrats have found success by connecting *any* issue to the one that's always affected us most.

Take, for instance, voter registration and the accusation that Republicans are "suppressing the black vote."

While there have been some legitimate attempts to suppress votes by a small number of both Republicans and Democrats (for instance, ridiculous redistricting or moving a polling place miles away from where most people in the district live), the main target for Dems is the notion that asking for an ID at the ballot box is "racist." You need an ID to cash a check, buy cough medicine, get your welfare check, or borrow a book. Yet no one goes around calling librarians a bunch of racists.

This voter ID thing isn't about genuine voter suppression. It's simply another emotional bogeyman crafted by the Democrats to keep black voters angry at the Republicans. It's a fallacy, an *emotional* fallacy, meant to keep the Dems in power. The real threat of *voter fraud* in the black community is far more troubling than the emotional deception of voter suppression. Former Alabama congressman Artur Davis has admitted as much. "When I was a congressman," he said, "I took the path of least resistance on this subject for an African American politician. Without any evidence to back it up, I lapsed into the rhetoric of various partisans and activists who contend that requiring photo identification to vote is a suppression tactic aimed at thwarting black voter participation." Now he supports such IDs.

The Heritage Foundation, led by black conservative Kay Coles James, maintains a voter fraud database that details more than one thousand proven instances of fraud convictions across the country. In one case, the mayor of Appalachia, Virginia, and his accomplices traded beer, cigarettes, and pork rinds to underclass citizens for votes and then stole absentee ballots out of the mail. In a town of only 585 ballots cast, 80 were proved fraudulent. The mayor and fourteen co-conspirators all went to prison. Another case, from 2012, involved former mayor Ruth Robinson, who attempted to rig her own reelection in Martin, Kentucky, by targeting poor and disabled residents, who were threatened with eviction from public housing if they didn't sign absentee ballots already filled out by Robinson. She was later sentenced to ninety months in prison for civil rights offenses, vote buying, and identity theft.

Where, then, is the *real* threat to disadvantaged voters?

And who are the real culprits?

I'M GOING TO let you in on a little secret.

There are many conservative African Americans. Men and women who support Republican policies; men and women who

despise the Democrats, who feel they've been taken advantage of for decades. Others who think the Democrats are "just as racist" as the Republicans—some even more so—but are still, somehow, the best option. *What am I gonna do,* they wonder, *become a Republican?*

It's a hidden conversation among people within the black community. They may agree with Republican policies when talking to someone face-to-face. But they don't dare share those feelings outside the room, and they *definitely* don't go out and say it on Fox News. (I'll probably get some guff for even putting it in this book.) The same people who agree with me in private conversations will fight me tooth and nail on social media because they cannot allow conversations conducted within the community to get into the public sphere. We don't want "the others" to know. So we keep our beliefs close to the vest and support those who pretend to be our allies (e.g., the Clintons). It's the cost of doing business.

When I started questioning this orthodoxy, I understood that I would likely put myself in a negative situation with my family and friends. I suspected I might lean far more Republican than I ever could have imagined, but if I was going to survive, I recognized I needed a support system. I needed to find more like-minded people. Others who identified as conservatives. As Republicans.

Which was not an easy thing to do where I lived.

I first reached out to a very outspoken Republican co-worker. Judge Dennis Greene was an administrative law judge at the agency I worked for, and also a notoriously staunch conservative. He loved talking politics and current affairs. However, because he was "old, white, and Jewish," many at work assumed he was a racist because of his conservative views. Colleagues actually went so far as to warn me not to even *discuss* politics with him. However, I knew I'd found a real-life Republican to talk with—which, in inner-city Chicago, is like spotting Bigfoot—and I wasn't going to miss the opportunity.

When I told Judge Greene I was thinking about joining the party, he assured me it was "the way to go." Desiring more information and perspective from someone I trusted, I asked the judge about current news. I wanted to educate myself on conservative thought and the ways of Republicans, considering I'd never been around any. How did they think, and why did they think that way? We talked about everything going on that year, from the Great Recession and healthcare reform to the shooting at Fort Hood, Texas, and the troop surge in Afghanistan. We talked about Pfizer's $2 billion fraud settlement, stem cell research, and Senator Arlen Specter switching parties to become a Democrat. I also elicited his take on the free market, capitalism, civil liberties, and even race. Judge Greene always gave me an earful about his outlook and, more significantly, the facts he'd used to get there.

He showed me that "conservatism" is much more than a label or an oversimplification of the policies driven by one political party. It's an approach to life. Its ideals often play out in policies, because that's where ideals become actions, but conservatism is ultimately about these timeless principles.

Another guy I spoke politics with was the building's security guard. Gustavo was from the Dominican Republic and, I discovered, very conservative. I went to him for my daily dose of discussion about local legislation, government, and culture. We discussed Obama's presidency, the swelling unemployment rate in Chicago, and the ongoing scandal with Illinois's Democratic governor, Rod Blagojevich, who'd been impeached for attempting to sell Obama's vacated Senate seat. I was learning about conservatism from an immigrant perspective and was surprised to discover that Gustavo was just as upset about illegal immigration as Judge Greene. He took great pride in being in the United States and respecting our system of laws. The immigration discussion was one I could connect to, given the problems discussed among members of my own family.

Having finally come to understand what a Republican was, and now beginning to see myself as one, I started evaluating the people closest to me. I knew I had "conservative values," but, I realized, so did many others in my family and community.

My grandfather, I now fully grasped, had always been a very conservative guy. A churchgoing man who started his own business and didn't want government in his life in any way. He often talked about immigration issues, taxes, and regulation, but now I listened to his concerns with more awareness, recalling how upset he got when the government tried to squeeze him for more money due to new laws he saw as being unfair to business owners. He was also an anti-union guy, believing that organized labor hadn't truly helped African Americans.

Politically, I now understood, he probably aligned with the Republicans. Yet he refused (for the reasons I've outlined) to become one himself. If you asked him, he'd have told you he was a Democrat, but it puzzled me that his beliefs never truly lined up with his professed political party.

Each night, this "stone-cold Democrat" would watch Bill O'Reilly on Fox News, and it seemed like he agreed with many of O'Reilly's points. Even so, he'd never align himself with "those racist Republicans."

And so I went through months of soul-searching.

Am I really one of those guys?

Having been programmed to believe something for so long, conditioned to buy into a specific narrative, I was shocked to find out it wasn't true. I experienced an array of emotions in those months. Depression was one. But there was also curiosity. And surprise. *What will people think about me if I come out publicly as a Republican?* I even tried to figure out if there was a way to keep my beliefs but somehow stay a Democrat, like my grandfather, whom I trusted as my dearest mentor.

That would have been the easiest route, the path that lots of people took. I won't pretend that I didn't consider it.

Instead, I told a few "safe" people around me that I was thinking I wanted to become a Republican and that whatever future political path I had lay with that party. The looks and responses I received—even from trusted friends and family— made me decide to keep it a secret a bit longer.

Until I knew more. Until I got deeper into party politics.

Until I knew what to do with the fear.

IF YOU'RE WHITE AND REPUBLICAN, you might face the discomfort of being labeled "racist." It's a terrible experience. But if you're *black* and Republican, you'd better get ready for a whole new echelon of terrible.

Condoleezza Rice, says the black community, is an *"Auntie Tom."* As a reward for being such a "sellout to her own race," she was even invited into the "Whitey Club" and given a membership to the (until then) all-male Augusta National Golf Club. And, as the actor and activist Harry Belafonte infamously quipped, Colin Powell, her predecessor as secretary of state was "permitted to come into the house of the master, as long as he would serve the master according to the master's plans." The black community looked at two of the most respected African Americans in U.S. history and basically called them house slaves.

Of the hundred-plus justices appointed to the U.S. Supreme Court, only *two* have been black—yet the second, conservative justice Clarence Thomas, doesn't even get a mention in the National Museum of African American History and Culture. A man who rose from a house in Georgia with no indoor plumbing to Yale University, and then on to the highest court in the land, apparently doesn't count as a noteworthy part of African American history. Anita Hill, the woman who, during his confirmation hearings, accused him of sexual harassment, *is* celebrated in the museum.

Edward Brooke, the first African American to be popularly elected to the U.S. Senate, was a Republican. (Hiram Revels was elected by the state legislature. Popular election of senators didn't become law until the Seventeenth Amendment was ratified in 1913.) So was Cora Brown, the first African American woman elected to a state senate. More recently, Michael Steele accomplished great things as the first African American chairman of the Republican National Committee. None of these "traitors" are celebrated in the National Museum of African American History and Culture either. Steele says that in his race for the U.S. Senate, he was often "painted in blackface with big red lips" and called an "Uncle Tom." He also had Oreo cookies thrown at him. Tim Scott, a black Republican senator from the "racist" state of South Carolina, has been called a "house negro" and a "disgrace to the black race" by other African Americans for years. And Gloreatha Scurry-Smith, a former Republican congressional candidate in Florida, had her entire face whitewashed with spray paint on billboards.

Myself? Having my opinions and concerns heard by millions on TV or in print is a blessing, but I, too, have been called an "Uncle Tom," a "coon," a "race traitor," and a "house nigger," along with many worse things. And some of these comments on social media and in email messages have come not from strangers, but from people who actually know me. As you can imagine, I no longer have relationships with those people.

The negative connotations associated with black Republicans are discriminatory, marginalizing, and meant merely as another attempt to control. Whether it's black folk using pejorative terms or white liberals making more passive-aggressive remarks (and some flat-out racist remarks), it's all based on a false pretense: that only Democrats (black or white) care about the well-being and advancement of the black community.

Back before I publicly announced as a Republican, I knew this was a fallacy because I cared about the well-being and advancement of the black community, but I also knew I was a conservative.

And I knew I had to get outside of my own community to find more answers and figure out my next step.

Eventually, in 2009, I reached out to the chairman of the Illinois Republican Party via Facebook. I sent a message. No response. Two months later, I tried again. Had I not done so, my journey might have ended right then and there, but I was curious and driven, and I wasn't going to give up after one try. I put a message on the party's Facebook wall, told them I was interested in learning more about the party and needed a mentor. This time, someone wrote back.

At a Starbucks, I met up with a woman named Rachel, chair-woman of the Naperville Township Republicans. Sitting down with a white Republican woman to drink $4 coffee (I went with hot chocolate) and discuss politics? I was definitely not in Kansas anymore. Or, rather, not in Englewood where the thought of politics in Chicago's most dangerous community started. I had no idea what to expect. Maybe she wouldn't care about all the reading I'd done, the conversations I'd sought out. Maybe . . . I wouldn't be accepted. Thankfully, Rachel treated me well, but she did have questions about why I wanted to make this big step, especially after she learned about my background.

A week later, I found myself driving to a Republican meeting in Naperville, a mostly white Chicago suburb located an hour west of the neighborhood where I grew up. It was June and already humid, but I was dressed to the nines, in my very best Sunday suit and tie, a proud twenty-one-year-old black man; a man who'd risen up from a childhood of poverty on the South Side of Chicago to become an educated, motivated citizen determined to succeed in a career in politics.

Let's be honest. A black man was at that time the president of the United States. And he'd started as a "community organizer" on the very same streets I'd grown up on. With that knowledge and inspiration, I held my head high as I walked toward the local chapter of "my party," heading to a GOP meeting for the first time.

The community center was a modest building right beside city hall. I followed the signs for the meeting and entered eagerly. The room was packed—and everyone in it was white. A whole lot of khaki and golf shirts. As I entered, thirty-plus older white heads turned toward me. A sense of surprise and confusion filled the room, and then they all returned to their conversations. I retreated to the continental breakfast in the back of the room: coffee, doughnuts, a nice spread.

Rachel greeted me, then Gary V., the former chairman of the Naperville Republicans, introduced himself to me. Gary was a really nice guy who made me feel welcome from the first minute. Apart from them, only a few of the others stopped by to welcome me. This left me as surprised as they'd all seemed to be when I first walked in. In previous situations I'd experienced in politics, people usually came up to me to say hello. I was usually the youngest person in the room, a pleasant and reassuring novelty. Likewise in this situation, I was the youngest person by well over a decade, but no one except Gary seemed to care.

What's wrong, guys? I said to myself. *You've never seen a black Republican before?*

People took their seats as the meeting began. It was hard not to hear the mumblings. "What's this black kid doing in the room?" "Who *is* he?" "Why the hell is he here?"

I sat there quietly, checking that my tie was straight, trying to focus on the various speakers, who were now spouting a variety of anti-Obama rhetoric mixed with calls for genuine community outreach.

Suddenly, a trucker-type dude with a big white mustache popped up in the front row, brandishing a large sign. "Impeach Obama!" he yelled in a crazed voice.

Now it was me who mumbled: "What the hell?" I could only imagine what was printed on the sign.

Rachel stood up and spoke in a soothing voice. "Charlie . . . Charlie. You need to stop interrupting the meeting." My new "GOP brother" sat back down, and I could tell this was not his first rodeo. The meeting continued with talk of local races, city council and state reps, upcoming elections, knocking on doors.

Then Charlie popped up again. "Obama's a terrorist! He's a Muslim!"

He had another sign. A *different* sign. I craned my neck to try to see where he was pulling them all from. *My God,* I thought. *My friends and neighbors were right. These people are crazy . . . and dangerous!*

This time, Rachel was not as contained. "Charlie!" she snapped. "If you interrupt this meeting one more time, I will remove you! You do this *every* week!"

It was like a *Saturday Night Live* sketch of a GOP meeting.

When the meeting was over, some of the polo-shirted members (the same men who'd glared at me earlier) came up to apologize for not welcoming me more warmly and for Charlie's behavior. Honestly, I was not deterred by the circus, or the initial hostility. I'd known hostility and hardship my entire life, and I wasn't going to let a couple of older white guys and a crazy dude with a ridiculous mustache deter me from my mission.

All through the summer, I kept driving back out to the meetings to further engage with Republican Party members, hopeful that one day I would be fully embraced. Charlie caused a scene at almost every meeting. And many of the members never warmed up to me. They clearly felt uncomfortable with my being there. The feeling was mutual. For too long, I did not *feel* like I belonged there. But I *knew* I did.

Eventually, some members' coldness morphed into suspicion. Confused, I approached the guy who'd been most welcoming: Gary V. "What's everyone's problem?" I asked.

"To be honest with you, Gianno . . . they think you're a spy for the Obama campaign. Sent by the Democrats of Cook County."

I must have laughed. (Some years later, while working on

the front lines for Mitt Romney's presidential campaign, I'd hear the same accusation.) But, as ridiculous as that was, their suspicions made sense. What other possible explanation was there for a young black man from inner-city Chicago to associate with a party that the black community believed to be racist and working to marginalize black people?

Of course, I was *not* there to observe and report back to Obama headquarters. (I imagine a secret bunker somewhere deep in Wakanda.) I was there because I'd become a steadfast believer in the party. But these people had been fed all the same expectations and lies as I had growing up.

I was not dissuaded from my goal. I saw an opportunity to make a legitimate impact and share my insight on why it was necessary for the Republicans to go after black votes, why it made sense for the black vote to become more competitive. I stayed on because I wanted to provide a voice for African Americans within the party. I also wanted ultimately to reach out to other blacks whose core beliefs and goals meshed with mine.

That summer, I began volunteering for the GOP.

By 2011, I'd become the director of African American outreach for the DuPage County Republicans and was working as a legislative aide for a statewide elected official. In this role, I'd travel down to the Illinois State Capitol in Springfield to meet with legislators, consultants, and government officials of all stripes. I'd talk with Democrats and Republicans. (Though it was mostly Democrats. Let's face it, I was still in Illinois.)

I'll never forget my first conversation with one colleague, a black Democrat who'd been charged with showing me around the capitol. When she first met me, she was shocked. "Oh," she said. "You're a brother . . . *and* you're Republican." When she'd seen my name, she'd assumed I was an Italian guy from Chicago. Despite her initial surprise, she received me warmly. In fact, most of the African American Democrats in the legislature wanted to work with me. Interacting with a young black Republican from the South Side of Chicago struck them as a unique opportunity, and they believed we could all do some good together. For the first time, I felt accepted as a Republican by black people.

THE BACKLASH to my GOP affiliation from friends and family, however, came almost immediately. Family members shunned me and treated me like I had a contagious disease. I "wanted to be white so badly," they said, I'd decided to make it official by joining the GOP. "Those white people" would use me up and then "lynch me when they were done with me."

Lynch me? Really?

The resentment and anger were intense. And distressing.

My social life even dried up. Young black women wanted nothing to do with me when they found out I was a Republican. My conservative views never seemed to bother them before, but things changed when those views got connected to the GOP. When it came up in conversation, at first they'd think I was joking, but when I started to explain my reasoning, the rejections were quick and clear. "Oh, you're one of *them.*" They weren't going to date some guy who hung out with those "racist Republicans."

So I started hanging out more with white friends and co-workers. I began to accept the "us versus them" mentality because I'd been rejected by my family and supposed friends for joining the party. That situation, being rejected by my own people, was hurtful. Still, I wanted to remain a voice for the black community within the GOP, even if it meant distancing myself from the community I'd set out to serve.

I want to be clear: The idea that black Republicans want to "be white" or "be loved by white people so they join the GOP" is a dismissive, hurtful fallacy.

But I *do* understand why many continue to perpetuate this narrative.

I did enculturate a little too much. "Uncle Tom" might even apply.

I did, specifically, enjoy having new white friends. Going on dates with white women who didn't reject me because of my politics. It was, I admit, like an award having white people . . . accept me.

"You're black . . ." some actually said. "But not like them."

Them.

I shudder now, but I must confess that at twenty-two, I saw this horribly racist remark as a badge of honor. I'd been raised in a rough environment: the gangbangers and addicts, the kids going nowhere, the blocks of Chicago that look like a "third world country." It felt good to be separated from that crowd for the first time in my life.

In a song about his future son, Kanye West wrote, "I might make him become Republican so everyone knows he loves white people." I think about that song when I remember those years after I first joined the party. Feeling rejected by my friends and family because of my conservative values—values several of them shared—while some on the right welcomed me with open arms and respect. I can hear the cries now as I did ten years ago: *They only opened their arms so they can use you to prove they're not racist. They want to say, "See? Here's a black person that's somewhat like me."*

Maybe. I don't know. I don't believe that was the case, but I certainly don't know others' intentions. I only know mine.

My mission was always to be a voice for African Americans within the party. An idea that has developed over time, but my goal has always been the same. And when friends and family told me to get over Lincoln Republicans and "ancient history" from a hundred years ago, and said things like "They're not like that now!" I simply replied: "*I'm* not ancient history. I'm a member of the party, and I'm here right now."

Years later, when I worked as a federal lobbyist to save a small South Side safety-net hospital (one that served thousands of low-income African Americans) from bankruptcy, or helped pass the First Step Act in Congress, freeing thousands of African Americans who'd been incarcerated for minor drug crimes, I knew I'd chosen the right path.

Following my conservative ideals and discovering my own political party was not easy. It cost me family, many sleepless nights, and even a canceled date or two. Throughout, I was well aware that my political affiliation would generate ire and confusion in the black community and beyond.

In "The Allegory of the Cave," Plato presents a metaphoric prisoner who escapes from a cave full of prisoners held by the bonds of false impressions and understanding crafted by others and also by their own doing. For these prisoners, it's far easier to accept the info readily given as reality. The road to true knowledge and empowerment for the escapee proves arduous and painful, a journey filled with missteps and confusion, but also growth and self-reflection.

It is not a process that happens overnight or in a single year. My own journey began more than a decade ago and continues today. But each step I take, I walk with the self-assurance and strength that comes from knowing I've chosen values that have stood the test of time and principles that are at the core of who I am as a person. Although I didn't understand it at the time, these values naturally first took root when I was a child. When I could see firsthand what the path too many others chose offered. When I first realized that if I was ever to have a life beyond mere survival, there was, for me, no other choice.

CRASHING THE PARTY

WHAT TO DO WHEN YOU'RE THE ODD MAN/WOMAN OUT

Recent studies suggest that as many as half of us will choose a different political party than our parents. You may live or work around people who assume they know what your political affiliations are, or who expect you to toe the same line as everyone else. But the truth is, you hold an entirely different viewpoint— a viewpoint you want to share. As uncomfortable as political conversations can be in today's volatile environment, it's never been more important for these conversations to take place among family, friends, and associates. Don't give in to the temptation to deflect such conversations or steer them into safer waters. Talking politics may be one of the last taboos in polite company, but it's a taboo you can overcome with the right approach. Don't fear the family dinner! The next time you have the opportunity, share your viewpoint and spark candid, meaningful conversation about the political beliefs and perspectives that are important to you. By keeping these tips in mind, you can effectively share your political positions—while keeping your relationships solid.

Don't change someone's mind. Rather, share your viewpoint. The biggest mistake we make in political conversations is to believe we'll change someone's mind on the spot. We won't. The absolute best-case scenario is that you'll make them think about what you say and perhaps question their own beliefs. Then, if you're *really* persuasive, they'll possibly decide to educate themselves further, often well after your conversation. You may never know the impact you have . . . and that's okay. You're not here to "educate"; you're simply sharing your own viewpoint.

Stay well-informed. When you're presented with questions, you're going to want to be able to provide answers and info that is solidly researched and easily understood. With the current twenty-four-hour news cycle, it's critical to stay well-informed on the latest developments in the political arena. But if you're genuinely looking to represent your political beliefs, keeping up with breaking news isn't your only job. Take the time to become well versed in the history of the political party or issue you favor. Understand its origins and the philosophies of its founders, as well as how those philosophies have possibly changed over time. As a successful thought leader, the more you can demonstrate the importance of the day's news within the context of the greater beliefs of your party, the stronger your position will be.

Don't assume people will agree—or disagree—with you. Assumptions in any conversation are dangerous, but they become particularly so when the subject turns to politics. Some of the most die-hard conservatives could have surprisingly liberal viewpoints in certain areas, and the most socially left-wing people you know could display surprisingly right-wing fiscal opinions. Present your points with an open mind, and pay attention to nonverbal cues to see who is more (or less) receptive to your ideas than anticipated. Keep an open mind.

R.E.S.P.E.C.T. There's a lot of talk these days about civility, and the loss of it, and for good reason. The art of conversation takes both practice and patience. Rather than allowing someone else to have their say, it's far easier to discount their opinions, call them names, cut them off, interrupt them, or deliberately ask pointed and argumentative questions to throw them off their game. By respecting and encouraging open dialogue, you will make far more of an impression on your audience than you can possibly imagine. Also, avoid the easy out of making blanket statements or overgeneralizing. Flat declarations like "All Democrats are . . ." or "Everyone who voted for Trump is . . ." are sure ways to undermine your position and get your audience to tune out. Politics has never been more nuanced or complicated than it is today, and others' beliefs have those nuances as well.

Don't take it personally. It's human nature to want others to agree with you and to feel affronted when they don't, particularly when you feel strongly about your opinions. But political discussions often get derailed when emotions are involved. Understand that not everyone will agree with you, even if—or especially if—you feel you're completely in the right, and don't let that disagreement undermine your state of mind. By keeping your cool, even in the face of disagreement or an emotional response by others, you'll maintain a strong position in the conversation.

Don't try to predict the future. If there's one thing the Trump administration has taught us, it's that the state of politics can change in a heartbeat. Don't fall into the trap of making declarations about the future that can be derailed by events you can in no way expect or predict. No matter how much you believe that you simply *know* what's going to happen in the next vote, the next election, and so on, keep your conversation on what is happening today—not tomorrow.

Above all, listen. Too often, people engaged in a political "discussion" care more about being heard than understanding an opposing viewpoint. Don't fall into that trap. Rather than mentally composing your own next declaration while the other person is talking, listen carefully and then repeat what you think the person has said back to them. This "reflecting" technique is a fantastic way to validate your conversation partner's perspective—and to ensure you truly understand it.

2

THE OTHER AMERICA

THE FOUNDATIONS OF INNER-CITY DESPAIR

EACH NIGHT, snipers positioned along the rooftop pulled on their military-grade night vision goggles, looking for enemies as far as a mile away. During the day, they studied torture techniques and hacked into the signals of local radio stations, broadcasting warnings and marching orders to hundreds of team members who were spread out across the city.

They called their headquarters "The Castle."

It was sixteen stories high, the tallest building for miles. The group's leadership was protected deep within. Anyone who entered the structure was patted down by armed guards. If someone protested, they were beaten. And if an enemy was found trying to enter the building, they were killed immediately.

If you think I'm talking about war-torn Syria or some Hollywood movie, you would be wrong. This was, rather, my home.

The Randolph Towers. A Chicago Housing Authority complex near the intersection of Sixty-third Street and Calumet Avenue. We lived in apartment 1107. Government housing. Two bedrooms, four kids to a room. We moved in when I was eight years old. My mother could not afford anything else.

Several years earlier, a Chicago gang called the Black Disciples had taken over the entire complex. It was centrally located in the neighborhood and housed some of the poorest people in Chicago. The poverty created an environment where people were willing to become pack workers, transporting and selling drugs. Guys were prepared to join the gang and become killers if called upon. The Black Disciples would drive up every afternoon in their twin Bentley cars, coming from somewhere else— somewhere nice where they all lived. They ran their operations well into the night, making as much as $50,000 a day from sales of crack cocaine and heroin in the building and $300,000 a day from their entire operation. Tenants could remain in the building only if they submitted to being regularly searched and sometimes assaulted. If they would not, the gang would run them out. Gunfire from rival gangs was a constant possibility. There were bullet holes in the concrete walls out front.

The police knew about all of this, but they rarely came into The Castle. They recognized it would take the U.S. Army's First Armored Division to successfully clean out the bad guys. One night, the gang's guards discovered an undercover cop on the premises. They shot him just outside the apartments as he tried to escape. His blood stayed on the concrete for weeks. Everyone, including the cops, knew who controlled the building.

Meanwhile, conditions inside deteriorated every year. My own bedroom walls were made of cinder blocks, but you could still hear the various fights and threats and babies crying all day and night. The elevator was usually broken. The garbage chutes outside every apartment were choked and unusable, home to thousands of roaches and an odor that made you gag. If you re-moved the medicine cabinet in the bathroom, you could crawl through to the adjoining apartment. Protective "fencing" lined the hallways, with the apartments on one side and open air on the other, with a chain-link barrier in between. It was the fenced hallways—more than the gangs, violence, and fear—that shamed me most. It felt like we were living in a cage.

Because, in reality, we were.

ON JANUARY 8, 1964, President Lyndon B. Johnson delivered his State of the Union address two months after winning a land-slide victory. Minutes into his speech, Johnson introduced what would become one of his signature policy initiatives. "Many Americans live on the outskirts of hope—some because of their poverty, and some because of their color, and all too many be-cause of both . . . ," he said. "This administration today, here and now, declares unconditional war on poverty in America."

At the time, Johnson and the Democrats enjoyed a rare 2-to-1 majority in both the House and the Senate. If they wanted to institute their agenda, now was the time to do it. Their War on Poverty became a major aspect of the government's Great Soci-ety program, a bevy of legislative and executive policies meant to help the "other America," those who failed to realize the ben-efits that a majority of citizens enjoyed in the middle-class eco-nomic expansion that followed World War II. Martin Anderson, an economist at Stanford University, has called the War on Pov-erty "the most ambitious attempt to redistribute income ever undertaken in the United States."

Estimates indicate that in the more than half a century since the program's passage, federal and state governments have spent $15 to $20 *trillion* to eliminate poverty in the United States. That's a lot of money. In comparison, the entire twenty-year war in Vietnam cost less than $1 trillion (adjusted for today's exchange rate), and the Iraq War cost just north of $2 trillion.

So it's fair to ask, more than fifty years later: What, exactly, did those noble and concentrated efforts to address poverty accomplish?

In 2017, the U.S. Census Bureau determined that 12.3 percent of Americans, or 39.7 million people, still lived below the poverty line. In 1964, the percentage was about 18 percent. While advocates might argue that a 6 percent reduction in poverty means the effort succeeded, others might claim, reasonably, that the cost of those programs should have delivered better returns.

Beyond the money spent, however, there was another, far greater unexpected cost: the quality of life for the very people Johnson hoped to help.

While Johnson and his fellow Democrats may have acted with the best intentions, they paved the road to generational poverty and disenfranchisement, brick by brick, in cities across America. As Ronald Reagan warned, "The nine most terrifying words in the English language are, 'I'm from the government, and I'm here to help.'" This observation had everything to do with the way Johnson's programs played out in reality.

During the 1970s, '80s, and '90s, welfare dependency *rose.*

Unemployment in the inner city rose.

More black men ended up in jail than ever before.

Fewer black students were graduating college.

More black children were being born out of wedlock (25 percent born to unmarried parents in 1960 versus *80 percent* in 2017).

More than fifty years later, the War on Poverty has become the longest-running war in American history. And Johnson's Great Society has become something out of a dystopian novel.

WHEN I WAS GROWING UP, our lights, gas, and water often got shut off after we fell behind on the bills. One time, after our gas went out, we resorted to boiling water in a pressure cooker for meals and for cleaning. My little sister Ashley, who was about eight, had boiled some water to take a warm bath. As she picked up the pressure cooker to pour the hot water into the tub, it slipped and spilled over her entire body. She suffered third-degree burns on her arms, legs, and thighs. I can still see the skin hanging off her, like an overcooked piece of chicken.

Months later, we were living with my grandmother when my mother came into my room and collapsed onto a chair beside the bed. I have a vague memory of ironing my shirts, no doubt trying to bring some order to my world. I tried to remain focused on the task at hand, but this was clearly a night when my mother was on one of her drug binges. She pulled a blanket over herself, and I could see that she was shaking. She was high—I knew how to spot that by now—but tonight I noticed something else. She was sobbing and fumbling with her hands beneath the blanket.

"Mom, what are you doing?" I finally said. She didn't answer, so I stepped over to her and raised the blanket. It was splattered with blood.

A box cutter in her hand, she'd been cutting her wrist. She was attempting suicide right in front of me. For her, a life in the inner city—a life with no real direction, no value; a life now completely dependent on the assistance of others—was no longer a life worth living.

I ran into the next room to get my grandmother. "She's trying to kill herself!" I yelled.

My grandmother shouted my mother's name, pleaded: "What are you doing? What are you doing?" She turned to me. "Call the ambulance!"

I share this story not to shock you, but because in inner-city America, such hopelessness and violence are daily possibilities. Everyone around me at the time had a parent who'd overdosed, a cousin or brother who'd been shot, a friend who was addicted to heroin, a father who'd put a gun in his own mouth. And we all knew that our friend, brother, or mother could be next. And we now see this continuing in places like the suburbs, where families are being destroyed by addiction to opioids. For too long, our country has been fighting the war on drugs without tangible results. Our elected officials must unite and bring sensible solutions to stop the pain that many have experienced in the inner city, the suburbs, and rural America.

My good friend Benjamin Hodges grew up with similar experiences in St. Louis. He recently moved to L.A. to pursue his career and works as a consultant to one of the largest defense contractors in the world. But he lived in the Blumeyer housing projects of St. Louis for much of his childhood.

Ben's mother, having recognized the dangers of government housing, moved the family out of the projects, despite not having the money to live anywhere else. As a result, they often went through stints of homelessness. When Ben was eleven, his entire family got evicted from their home—not because they hadn't paid rent, but because their landlord hadn't used their rent to pay *his* mortgage. "We had barely twenty-four hours to vacate," Ben recalls, "and spent all that night packing up as many things as we could to get into storage." The sheriff showed up the next day with three guys and proceeded to move their furniture out onto the street, in the rain. "I was humiliated," he says. "We all were."

His family landed in a shelter while his mom saved money to rent another home. Mere days from making that goal a reality, Ben's stepfather, a recovering addict, took every dime she'd saved and spent all of it on crack cocaine. "My mom couldn't bear to look us in the eyes all that week," he says. "And we were homeless again, with no money . . . again."

Do I blame LBJ for this? For Ben's stepfather? For the callous sheriff? For my own mother's suicide attempt that night, and the ones on other nights to come? Do I blame LBJ for my parents not being together? For the armed drug lords I had to pass every day on my way to school?

No. People make their own choices.

But I also can't pretend that the choices of my mother and others weren't drastically altered by the intentions of our government—a government that all too often believes it can solve a problem simply by tossing money at it. Or, worse, by trying to control how others live.

My community didn't need handouts and rules to live a better life. Our needs were far more real. And, admittedly, more difficult to solve.

There were no drug rehabilitation services in our neighborhood. There were almost no jobs, as crime and overtaxation and overregulation had driven most businesses away. The police had largely surrendered the blocks to the gangs. The year I was born (1986), only twenty-one people in all of Chicago's public housing called 911 for help, even though crime was a daily reality for the thousands who lived in those projects.

There were also few fathers or even men in our neighborhood. Bill Clinton's 1994 crime bill included the stipulation that people with criminal records be denied access to public housing. We lived on the South Side of Chicago. Respectfully, how many black men between fifteen and forty do *you* suppose had a criminal record? A small bag of weed meant that a father or brother or son was no longer allowed in the home. The law of our land effectively separated families in a place where stability and family were needed most.

Tragically, in inner-city communities there remains a cycle of generational poverty. Now young girls have babies, hoping to escape dysfunctional family environments by getting on government assistance. Section 8 will get you a house, and other programs will provide you with food stamps, subsidies for utilities, and cash. In your mind, the government is taking care of you. But this is a dangerous illusion that keeps those living on the margins drowning in poverty, with no end in sight. Ultimately, they can no longer imagine any other world beyond the aberrant microcosm of the projects.

Even when some folk move into a better area, that conditioning moves with them. We could spend *$50 trillion,* handing each person a $1 million check, moving them out of the projects to a nice community—safer, cleaner, with manicured lawns. But they would still jack the car up on the lawn, let the oil drain into the street, not cut the grass, pile trash in the backyard. Their addictions would follow them. As would the notion that people who work or go to school are the weak ones, just putting on airs.

Because it's *not* about their new environment.

It's that they didn't change within themselves.

IN 1731, a member of the British Parliament, James Oglethorpe, proposed a bold idea for a new settlement between Carolina and Spanish-controlled Florida—a settlement specifically built for Britain's most disadvantaged citizens. (Oglethorpe himself had spent five months in debtors' prison.) His genuine hope was that "Georgia" would provide a new opportunity for the "worthy poor," and his plan included a methodically designed city to anticipate all the community's future needs. The colonists, most of whom had been selected from debtors' prisons, had no desire to do the work Oglethorpe had planned for the community and demanded the colony instead bring in slaves to do most of the work. Oglethorpe surrendered control of the colony in 1750 and returned to England broke. Slavery came to Georgia that same year.

In 1999, more than 250 years after Oglethorpe's original proposal, the CEO of the Chicago Housing Authority, Phillip Jackson, came up with a similar plan that also sounded like a great idea. He wanted to tear down the projects, to get rid of places like The Castle. They looked like cages and jails, he said. Instead of forcing people to live there, he'd give them housing vouchers and let them move into nicer communities and actual houses.

But some didn't want to leave. They didn't *want* to move out of the projects because that's where they'd grown up. It was home, community. It was the only place they could see themselves living.

In the end, people had no choice. The buildings came down, and in some cases the police had to go in and remove people physically from their homes. The projects—the violence and gangs and drugs and poor conditions—had become the only reality these people could envision. The world beyond was too complicated for them. They couldn't face it. And when their location did eventually change, by force or otherwise, they usually still lived like they had in the projects. In fact, that's largely why things became systemically more violent in the city of Chicago. People who'd been gang leaders in the projects started recruiting in their new neighborhoods—areas where people hadn't previously been involved in gangs.

Clearly, housing and checks aren't a stand-alone solution. People need job training, computer skills, and financial education to learn how to handle their money. But these skills must be connected to deeper, more personal values. In Barry Goldwater's seminal 1960 book, *The Conscience of a Conservative,* he explains that "the material and spiritual sides of man are intertwined; that it is impossible for the State to assume responsibility for one without intruding on the essential nature of the other; that if we take from a man the personal responsibility for caring for his material needs, we take from him also the will and the opportunity to be free."

Government can only do so much. Organizations can only do so much. People have to *want* the power that comes with personal responsibility, to even know that such capability and power exist. There is not one government handout that can pour into you the desire to better your own life.

In my experience, there are two kinds of people who get on government assistance.

There are those who get on it because they really don't have a choice. They despise being on it. Their pride is stricken. The notion that someone else is taking care of them feels demeaning. These people see government assistance as a temporary measure, as *assistance,* to merely help them get through a rough patch and get back on their feet.

That is how the system was created to work. There was some hope of this becoming a reality with the 1996 Welfare Reform Act—a bipartisan compromise between then–Speaker of the House Newt Gingrich and then–President Clinton—a welfare reform plan that significantly changed the nation's welfare system to require work in exchange for time-limited assistance. Its official name was the Personal Responsibility and Work Opportunity Reconciliation Act.

Personal responsibility.

When I first started working for the federal government as a teen, my work trainer was receiving the benefits of the Welfare Reform Act. It provided her with an opportunity to work a full-time job while still receiving her welfare benefits and at the same time learning valuable skills. In a matter of months— months!—she was able to get off the system entirely and continue working full-time.

But then there's the other folk.

They get on government assistance, get comfortable, and often figure out how to manipulate the system as much as possible so they can continue on that same pathway going forward. They seek to make this new arrangement as permanent as possible.

I've seen such thinking take down even the strongest of people. For years, my grandmother (on my mother's side) was our saving grace. She would visit our apartment in The Castle with bags of groceries and shoes that she bought from Payless. She tried to take care of us from afar, but eventually she had seen enough. "You need to move out of here," she said. "This is a bad situation."

My mom finally acquiesced. She headed to rehab across town, and my siblings and I moved in with Grandma. She was a no-nonsense woman of faith and industry. She was quick to set us straight but always made sure we were safe and provided for. Grandma worked ten hours a day as a private duty nurse, serving mostly wealthy clients. We were doing okay for a while, living in a more decent area of Chicago.

But that arrangement didn't last for long.

I still remember that day. Grandma left for work as usual that morning, but it wasn't long before she came back. She was trembling, eyes wide. "Somebody hit me," she cried, collapsing to the steps, hands to her neck. "They ran off."

She had been in a car accident, a hit-and-run, and it changed her life. The driver had been drunk. We found out later that he'd been in three other accidents the same day and had no insurance to speak of. Grandma's car was totaled, and her neck and back were not in much better shape.

This woman, who'd worked hard her entire life, could no longer do her job. Her back brought agony with every step. Weeks later, she tried to work a reduced schedule. She was now doing overnight shifts—harder on her life and well-being, but easier on her body—but then she couldn't even do that anymore. Despite her best efforts, within a year she'd lost her house, a house she'd owned for almost a decade. She probably could have kept it had she turned to us and said, "Okay, y'all are going into foster care." But she didn't. She had committed to caring for us. So we moved again. The government checks began to arrive again. Not for my mom anymore, but for my grandmother.

When you get into this dependency mentality, it changes everything.

You can be an individual who has worked your whole life, but once you begin to get on government assistance programs, your focus can . . . change. Your thought can become *How can I get more?* More housing, more food stamps, more cash, more assistance to pay for your lights and gas.

My grandmother's desire to work the system all too quickly took on a life of its own. People in the community would come around and say, "Listen, *these* are the kinds of things I've been pulling off to get more of this and that." And my grandmother would lean into it. I'm not saying she broke the law, but when you start engaging in this behavior, you completely lose your pride as you try to figure out how to survive by working the system. Even more tragically, you begin to pass down these tactics to your family and those around you.

There were times in my teens I was told *not* to work because it could jeopardize the government assistance our family was receiving. Even then, the idea was astonishing to me. Poverty and government dependence don't just affect your bank account. Eventually, they come to affect your mind. You make decisions you normally wouldn't make because you're trying to survive. Your mental state can become extremely limiting. You see nothing but what's in front of you. And when what's in front of you is a politician with another handout, watch out.

How many Americans have accepted the narrative that things will never get better and that only government handouts are the answer to all that ails? Too many.

When we lived in The Castle, gang members would try to recruit me. When I said no, they'd beat me. Worst of all, these same guys were my classmates at school. How many young people have joined such gangs not for the money or because they thought it would be cool, but rather for survival? To avoid being beaten or killed. Too many.

When Goldwater warned of the balance between "the material and spiritual sides of man," he understood that those trapped within government assistance would eventually devalue their own lives. So much so that life itself would take on little meaning. Thus, gangbangers ready to murder without hesitation, as easily as grabbing a bite to eat. Thus, an abortion rate much higher than the national average. Thus, mothers attempting to kill themselves with drugs and box cutters.

More often than not, the people around me weren't simply deciding to give up. They were living in a culture of dependency that had been passed down from birth. My mother and grandmother gave in to the culture. And they expected me to figure out the best way to live on that same track, to game the system and not even try to escape.

My friend Ben agrees. "Most of the time, what you see in the housing projects are *generations* of families," he says. "People accustomed to this lifestyle. It becomes comfortable, so they don't move away, and even their children stay and raise kids in the same environment." In neighborhoods like the ones where Ben and I grew up, there is no perceived incentive to advance. After all, the checks for housing and the food stamps and other assistance arrive every month.

This is why the system *must* be reformed. Welfare should exist only for a certain period of time, unless you're disabled and can't physically work. It should not last for a generation or more. There are millions of jobs open, without enough people to fill them or, rather, without enough people who have the necessary skills and training. This is where the government should come in, providing incentives for real-world training and educating recipients about a life beyond government dependence.

Many in such conditions often ask, "What about slavery?" or "What about racism?" They speak of a "five-pound bag" they're carrying: the institutional racism and generations of poverty that have made it tougher for them to succeed. We can't deny that racism has a genuine impact on inner-city (largely black) communities. However, citing racism as the *sole* reason for their lack of success is just another trap meant to keep underprivileged people wholly dependent on anyone but themselves.

To be clear, I understand and see the systems that have worked against me in life. But the moment I accepted that five-pound bag—that bag of *Oh, I'm not going to make it because I know these folk are racist. They won't give me a shot because of where I'm from or how I speak* and all the other reasons too many of us have been conditioned to use—I would have been done for. It's okay for me to acknowledge the barriers. But it is *not* okay for me to accept them as some unconquerable burden that leaves no possibility but for me to fail. Don't dare give me *that* bag.

A VARIETY OF FACTORS have hindered the elimination of poverty in America over the past fifty years. The conflict in Vietnam, racial unrest, "white flight" from cities to the suburbs, the decline of American industrial growth, black middle-class movement from urban centers, rampant economic decline in the agricultural South, and other issues all have blocked the possibility of a major decline in or total end to poverty in America.

The true tragedy is the loss of human dignity created by an environment of government dependence where self-reliance is rarely even presented as an option and all too often mocked.

I grew up in a household with eight siblings. Some have been to jail, and most are struggling with career and finances.

If I hadn't been around my paternal grandfather on the weekends—when I saw him earning a legitimate income, working hard, signing checks, going to the bank, reaching out to customers old and new, hiring workers, paying taxes, working with local politicians and businesses—I, perhaps, would be just as lost as the rest of my family.

How would the seed in me, that desire to start working, have been watered? Where do such qualities come from? Mine came from the examples of my grandfather and grandmother. For years, I watched my grandmother go off to work every day, even in great physical pain after her accident. And I felt good when my grandfather paid me $10 a day to hold the flashlight while he did his plumbing job. Earning that $10 every weekend meant the world to me. He was teaching me a work ethic, nurturing a burning desire to work, to earn money, to have control of my own success. The conditions I saw around me only motivated me to go beyond my present world. And there is one moment I remember when that spark of determination turned into a raging fire.

One day, I was getting dropped off at The Castle after spending the weekend with my father. My aunt was with us. As we pulled up to the building, we found ourselves in the middle of a high-speed chase. Three police cars, lights flashing, sirens wailing, were pursuing a car (a "steamer" as such cars were called, clearly just stolen) that spun onto the sidewalk in front of my home. Two men jumped out and ran into the apartment building as the police poured out of their cars and gave chase. Several had drawn their guns.

The guys must have caught a rare working elevator or made it into a friendly apartment because the police came back out of

the building minutes later. The men had escaped, and these officers weren't going door-to-door for sixteen floors to find them.
It was shocking they'd gone in at all.

I looked at my father and aunt, feeling humiliated about
where I lived. I'd never told them about the beatings I sometimes got on the way to school. Or the gangbangers who approached me as a recruit. I didn't tell them about the needles in
the hallways or bullet holes in the stairwells. Or how mom left
me with her "friends" while she went and did drugs, and then
brought men around. I guess I didn't have to.

I could see the pain in their eyes, but all three of us knew
there wasn't a thing to be done about it. I was supposed to live
with my mother. I stepped from the car and walked toward my
Great Society housing.

I am not a victim, I told myself with each step. *I'm getting out
of this hell.*

That was big talk for a little kid. But I meant every word.

3

DON'T LIKE WHAT'S GOING ON? CHANGE IT.

MOVING BEYOND LIBERAL DEPENDENCE

DURING THE 2016 presidential primaries, Bernie Sanders won more votes from Americans under age thirty than Hillary Clinton and Donald Trump *combined*. This shouldn't be that much of a surprise. Both Clinton and Trump brought a mountain of personal and professional baggage to their campaigns.

But there was something else going on.

Sanders ran a campaign based on promises of free college, free healthcare, guaranteed housing, more control over big business and banks, putting the rich "in their place," and government patronage from cradle to grave. These promises were appropriate, given his six decades spent as a passionate socialist. The surprise was that for the first time in American history, these once fringe beliefs had found a receptive audience.

According to recent Gallup polls, America's millennials— those, like me, who were born between 1981 and 1996—have soured on capitalism and the free market. Less than half of us

(45 percent) view capitalism in a positive light, and just as many carry a *positive* view of socialism. An even higher percentage of young Hispanics, Asian Americans, and African Americans view socialism positively.

Should those of us who still favor the free market and limited government be concerned? Surely this is just a bunch of thirtysomethings who are mad about still living at home or about their student debt. How much damage could they really do to the fabric of our country?

Plenty, actually. Millennials are now the biggest generation of Americans *ever.*

By pure numbers alone, we've surpassed the baby boomers, a generation that has dominated American thought, business, politics, and culture for more than fifty years. If the Democrats are able to cash in on this new megageneration that believes government control of industry, health, energy, education, and even Starbucks coffee will make for a better country, we could be in for a world of hurt. I can't help but think of Venezuela. For years, it was one of the most prosperous countries in the world, with a booming economy, but it was destroyed in less than a decade by radical socialist policies.

The left has convinced an entire generation of Americans, more of whom are living a middle-class (or better) life than ever before, that somehow the system that brought them that comfort is bad. In contrast, only 24 percent of baby boomers *ever* bought into the liberal mindset—even when they were young and idealistic and heading to San Francisco for the "Summer of Love."

So what happened? How did Alexandria Ocasio-Cortez, a Bernie acolyte who seemingly believes government is the solution to every social and personal ailment, become the face and voice of the Democratic Party and America's possible future? It has everything to do with the context in which millennials were raised.

Boomers grew up during America's economic golden years following World War II, when our competition in Europe and Asia was still largely in smoldering ruins. Millennials, my generation, grew up in a different time. We became voting adults during the economic collapse of 2008 and the sluggish economy of the Obama years. We graduated to an economy that had fewer jobs for white-collar workers and was even worse for those without a college degree. For the first time in a hundred years, Americans were statistically far less likely to earn more than their parents, and wages were not keeping up with inflation. The pensions that our parents and grandparents were offered in their thirties were a thing of the past. Healthcare costs doubled, then tripled. College, which one could pay for with a summer job in the 1970s, now costs an average of $20,000 a year.

During the Obama years, an entire cohort of Americans went to college and worked hard to graduate, but instead of getting their first job and apartment, they ended up in their parents' basement with a cashier job at Best Buy or Walmart. Today, a fourth of all young adults (ages twenty-five to thirty-five) are *still* living at home—twice the number as in 2005. Thanks largely to student loans, but primarily to credit card debt ("needing" things they can't yet afford). The average millennial already owes $42,000 in debt. More than a tenth of millennials owe more than $100,000, and half of them have some type of side hustle to make ends meet.

You would think this generation, more than most, would recognize the failures of an economy so recently strangled by overtaxation and government regulation. You would think this generation, specifically, would reject the pitfalls and ruin that come with government meddling and socialism.

For years, Republicans accused President Obama of being a "socialist," driven to destroy the free market that had made the United States the wealthiest nation, with the largest middle class, in human history. And with the way the economy stagnated during Obama's run, the proof of those GOP claims would seem to have been in the pudding. Yet Obama still left office with a 77 percent approval rating among millennials. If he was a socialist, my generation was evidently okay with that.

The Democrats, who've always had a stronger marketing and PR machine than the Republicans, ran with it. They convinced half a generation that the reason you don't have what you want in life is because this other guy—who's probably worked for thirty or forty years now, but we'll leave that part out—*he* has it! *He's* the only reason you're not living like a Kardashian! And you *should* have the same, or even more, regardless of the fact that you haven't actually done that much in life.

Liberals have taken the same invented bogeyman they've used with black America and started feeding it to young America. Why would anyone who buys this rubbish ever look at capitalism positively? It's far easier to hate the people "at the top."

This thinking, alas, isn't new. Following the Great Depression, the young Americans of the 1930s soon gave rise to a far more powerful and intrusive federal government. Many even went so far as to embrace communism. The Depression had scared them into possible self-destruction. The Obama years seem to have had the same effect.

When Alexandria Ocasio-Cortez ran for Congress, she was a bartender and waitress living with her mother. Eight years before, she'd graduated cum laude from Boston University with a degree in international relations and economics. Despite that degree and eight years to get her career going, she had less than $7,000 in the bank. She also—while arguing that banks should forgive *all* student loan debt—owed the U.S. Department of Education as much as $50,000 in student loans.

This situation, apparently, somehow wasn't a result of her own doing. Rather, it happened because—in her worldview—the boomers were holding her back from finding the right job. It happened because of white men. Because of the patriarchy. Because of the banks and big business and "rich people," who had a stranglehold on all the money and kept her from making her own fortune.

And it was the government alone that would make things fair for her, for everyone. Only it could solve all this perceived injustice. Solve private problems of staying out of debt, finding housing away from your parents, growing a career, building a nest egg, and so on. The government was the only one that could set things right and guarantee that the "pursuit of happiness" became, simply, "happiness."

More than anyone else, Ocasio-Cortez has become the personification of one path for millennials.

Meanwhile, I was on the other path.

FOR YEARS, Washington, D.C., was the place I wanted to live and work.

Having gone into politics at such a young age, I used to dream about what it would be like to move to the city of power. In 2010, I was twenty-three years old and trying to figure out how to get there. I started talking to people I'd met through the DuPage County Republican Party. These folk would do campaign trips and come to the district to work for their D.C. bosses in Congress. They all had what I wanted for myself, a connection on Capitol Hill.

I finally made a connection with a staffer on the Hill named Patrick and started asking him questions about D.C. He assured me I was "exactly what Capitol Hill was looking for" and that my ten years of experience in campaigning and government work would prove marketable. I, of course, was thrilled to hear this. I told him I was even willing to move there with no job if I had to as I'd built up a nest egg to get me through a couple months. I was willing to do whatever was necessary to make it, because that's how much I believed I could do great things in D.C.

Just before I was supposed to move to D.C. without a job, I received a call from a politician in Illinois who'd won a recent election. He had a possible job offer—but in Springfield, not Washington.

"You've made an impression with the party," he assured me, and he wanted to see if I was interested in working in his new office. At this point, D.C. was still my plan, but I was willing to take the meeting. I drove almost two hours downstate for a fifteen-minute meeting that ended up being an hour-long chat. A few days later, I was offered a job on his legislative affairs team.

It was a good job with good pay. A nice step in the right direction. Worst case, I thought, I could continue building connections in Washington and move there when the time was right.

The bulk of my days were now spent in the state capitol in Springfield, lobbying on behalf of this state office. It was an amazing time. I was breaking bread with some of the most powerful people in Illinois. Working with them to make a difference in the lives of others. It was truly an empowering feeling.

That said, I still had this nagging feeling I needed to be in D.C.

One evening, I called my girlfriend after a particularly rough day at work. I was pretty upset on the phone. My girlfriend was a successful ob-gyn, fantastic (albeit a little brusque at times) at giving professional advice. This night, she didn't disappoint. She listened to my complaints about work and then offered a comment that resonated far beyond the specific and immediate circumstances.

"What are you crying about?" she said. "If you don't like what's going on, change it."

It was that simple.

That's right, I realized. *If you don't like it, change it.* I could keep complaining for another five years, waiting for someone else to fix the problem, or I could take ownership of my own concerns and goals. Choose to be truly self-reliant.

In that moment, I made a decision. I would move to D.C.

Thanks, in part, to the work I'd done running African American outreach for the DuPage County Republican Party, I landed a job working for Mitt Romney's 2012 presidential campaign. The work involved traveling around the country as part of Romney's advance team. We managed press, fundraisers, rallies, and TV interviews. As campaign/press advance, I was in charge of the logistics for the campaign stops, from booking the venue to working with the Secret Service and ensuring that the press had everything they needed to cover the candidate. We traveled across the country, from New York to Florida, Ohio to Las Vegas, Pennsylvania to Washington State.

Being a guy from the inner city, I only really understood inner-city life. Even when I'd moved out to the suburbs of Chicago, I was still in the suburbs of a major city. Many Thanksgivings, I had the privilege of visiting Helena, Arkansas, where my grandfather had been raised. We had a tradition of going to spend time with our family there, which gave me a taste of the beautiful South. But I hadn't yet had the opportunity to see the rest of the country—the farms, the factories, the miles of suburbs—and to meet the people there.

Working for Romney, I quickly discovered how great so many other parts of this country are. I met amazing people. People who'd also been dismissed, their values trampled on or forgotten. People, like those I knew in Chicago, who'd been marginalized by the liberals who run the bigger cities, the liberals on the coasts who overlook—or, worse, mock—the "fly-over states."

When I wasn't on the road, I started making more connections in D.C. I needed to plan ahead. If Romney became president, I had a good shot at getting into the White House as . . . something. But if he lost, I needed somewhere to work after the campaign was done.

My plan had always been to work for one of the trade associations' lobbying firms or join a corporation as a federal lobbyist in D.C. While many may see "lobbying" as a dirty word, I believed it was the best path to effect real change. Having worked in politics for a decade, I now realized that the most powerful industry in the country was not media, banks, teachers, or scientists. It was lobbyists. Nowadays, if I don't like what a teacher is getting paid or what's going on in the media, I'll draft a bill to change it and get it into the right hands.

When I wasn't traveling for Romney, I was taking meetings and trying to get my foot in the door somewhere. I talked with chiefs of staff and people who ran offices of their own. I went to party fundraisers and took meetings at all of the biggest firms: KPMG, Deloitte, PricewaterhouseCoopers, national bankers, the realtors' association. For six months, I passed out cards, shook a thousand hands, and did follow-ups with everyone who responded. One guy who deserves a special shout-out is Yul Edwards, chief of staff for a Democratic congressman from the west side of Chicago. Yul was such a good guy. The first time I met him, he invited me to a GOP fundraiser and then to a fish fry at the DNC headquarters. (Fried *catfish,* too, my favorite meal.) Yul really opened up doors for me in Washington. The next few months were a blur of meeting new people. It was hectic and exhausting but needed to be done. Throughout, everyone was very much *Yeah, yeah, we'll do this and we'll do that,* but at the end of the day, no contracts or offers appeared in my inbox.

Then Romney lost to Obama.

I was without a job for the first time in ten years. I soon found myself on Capitol Hill, interning for free, taking calls for a congressman's staff. "Thank you for calling Congressman So-and-So's office. How may I serve you?" I was playing receptionist and doing tours for constituents, showing them around the capitol. All for free, while my bank account dropped to negative. I'd also started working with the congressman's legislative director, who would give me more substantive projects to work on. He'd say, "You were lobbying in Illinois, right? What do you need to do to get this information or do X, Y, Z?" I was calling staff and the people I used to work with. I also tapped into my government relations skill set by doing analysis and writing reports on different pieces of legislation. I started feeling good because I was doing work that was helpful and impactful.

But that period was also one of the most humbling experiences of my life. I ran through the rest of my savings, the money I had made on the Romney campaign and the nest egg I'd built prior to coming to D.C. At one point, I even applied to work as a straight-up receptionist at a trade association. They called, having looked at my résumé, and asked, "Why are you applying for *this* job?"

What could I say? I needed the money. I'd have shoveled fish guts if that was what it took to be successful.

And so, with a college degree and more than a decade of political and government experience under my belt, I found myself answering the telephone, taking messages, and making minimum wage for the first time in my life. I was also taking orders from people younger than me, some of whom had just graduated college. I had all this experience, having worked in politics since I was fourteen. Worked for the federal government for seven years. Worked as the director of government relations for a government agency, as a legislative adviser at the state level. Campaigned beside the GOP nominee for president of the United States. It seemed no one cared.

That being said, it never occurred to me to blame anyone else for this. Or to be resentful of what anyone else had. Rather, I worked my butt off and kept networking in D.C. as best I could. One advantage to that was that I started attending receptions where they had free food and drink—anything to save on the grocery bill.

Years before landing in D.C., I'd bought all sorts of nice suits and shoes and other clothes. Now I was returning them for cash.

One suit was more than five years old, and I drove an hour outside of town to return it to a store where they didn't know me so I wouldn't be embarrassed. They refused the return at first, since the suit was so old. But I had my receipt and argued my case before a couple of managers and eventually got the cash. It was crushing, but I needed the money to pay my rent.

Sometimes, shamed and mortified, I'd even pester a couple of friends and my godmother for some cash to stay afloat. I spent many nights just sitting in my apartment alone.

It was a sobering experience. Most people would have said, "To heck with this. I'm out, I'm leaving. Time to go back to Chicago." And those thoughts *did* cross my mind on many occasions. But I kept hearing God say, *Just trust me.* Still, when you're hungry and the cellphone's got zero bars, it's tough not to think *I made a mistake* or *Let me see what's going on elsewhere.*

As if someone heard those thoughts, I was offered a job in Chicago working for a high-level Illinois businessman. "What the hell are you doing in D.C.?" he asked after hearing I'd moved. When I told him what was going on, he replied: "Forget that. Come back to Chicago and work for me." He offered me a good salary and a chance to do the work I loved: lobbying and government relations. But it was back at the state level. I told him it sounded good but asked if he could let me sleep on it.

That same night, I sprang up in bed with a revelation. I called him the next morning. "Hey," I said. "Last night, I got the best idea you've ever heard. Why don't you start a D.C. office and, um, let me run it?" I laid out the whole plan for him, creating the perfect blueprint for federal government relations.

"No," he replied. "Come back to Chicago."

I declined his offer. No matter how much it seemed like I'd failed, I wasn't yet willing to give up my dream of making it in

D.C. I must have interviewed with a dozen companies, trying to get into government relations, but none of them took the bait. Then, just when I thought I had reached the lowest point, I had one more setback to absorb.

I'D GOTTEN AN INTERVIEW with Brownstein Hyatt Farber Schreck, one of the top lobbying firms in the country. There was a job opening in their energy regulatory government relations department—a job that would have been perfect for me, considering it meant engaging with the congressional committee the congressman I now interned for chaired. After my first interview, the woman who interviewed me said, "I've met with all the prospective candidates, and you, by far, are the best. You're this, you're that. You're absolutely my pick, and I'm the one hiring."

It was all I could do to stay in my chair.

"All we gotta do," she said, "is have you meet with the partner of the practice. A simple formality. I've already made the decision, though. You're our guy."

The recruiter I'd been working with called later that day and confirmed everything the woman had told me. "This is excellent!" she said. This was it. Things were finally happening. "I'm glad to see this, Gianno. You've hung in there so long," she said. "It's going to work."

I'm sure you know where this is going. We've all been there at one time or another.

The evening before my meeting with the partner, my recruiter called. "I don't know how to tell you this," she started, "but in thirty years of recruiting, I've never had this experience."

"What?" I grinned. "They just want to hire me outright? No second interview?"

"No," she said. "The partner of the practice, he . . . he said you have far too much experience. There's no need to even interview you. The offer's off."

The news hit me like a ton of bricks. I'd been willing to answer phones and sort mail for minimum wage, and it felt like it had gotten me nowhere. I prayed hard for days. How is it that I'm applying for all these jobs, coming this close, and not getting anything?

But in that moment of disappointment, my mind returned to a voice I'd been hearing in my head for months—a still small voice had been planting this idea . . .

Start your own firm.

I'd ignored it. I had almost no experience or contacts in D.C. In the lobby game, you work with different bodies: city, county, state, Congress, the White House. My lobbying experience ended at the state level. There were chiefs of staff who'd worked for powerful members of Congress, only to fail when they tried starting firms of their own. *How am I going to start off with less than them and be successful?* These were the doubts in my head. *No, no, no,* I thought. *I'm going to work for somebody first. Then, eventually, I'll leave and start my own thing.*

No, I heard again in my head and heart. *Start your own firm now.*

Finally, after months of hearing this and with nothing to lose, I decided: *Okay, I'm really going to do this. If no one else will hire me, I'll just make my own D.C. firm.*

I came up with a name and began creating a website. It was a start. I reached out to everyone I'd ever met—trade associates, corporations—and told them: "Hey, I'm starting a lobbying firm, and I'd love to get your business."

A lot of them looked at me like I was nuts. One guy, who worked with a top lobbying firm, took me out for dinner . . . and a warning. "Bro," he said. "Listen. . . . Not many people are going to tell you this, but I'm just going to be honest. You're not going to be successful. I appreciate all the hard work and what you're trying to do, but it's just not going to work. The best thing now is to try and get a staff assistant job on the Hill. Work your way up. Maybe in five, ten years, this will work. It takes more than a website and a smile, Gianno."

Staff assistant was one position above unpaid intern. No thanks.

I told him: "No, no. I'm doing it. I'm doing it."

When I tried to pick up the check as thanks for his advice, he just laughed and said, "You don't have any money, bro."

Others weren't as gentle with their advice. One guy, who'd worked as a senior lobbyist at a prominent national trade association, called me as soon as he heard what I was up to. "No one gives a fuck about your Illinois experience," he screamed into the phone. "Nobody's going to fucking hire you! You need to just go back to Chicago. No one gives a shit about you. You should just go home." The anger was tangible. And I barely knew this guy.

Who does that?

A lot of people. Co-workers, family, "friends."

They'd say: "Why would you even think about that?" or "What do you know about that?" Some, like that senior lobbyist, were just more straightforward with their negativity. Years before, though, I had learned that you'll never be criticized by someone doing *more* than you. Only by someone doing less.

From an early age, I wanted to better myself. In particular, I wanted a job in downtown Chicago. The tall buildings and nice restaurants, all that kind of stuff. And so I started working with more professional and educated people than those I'd known in The Castle. I even joined Toastmasters to improve my public speaking skills after a fellow intern, a white kid my age, was brave enough to tell me the truth when I asked him why I wasn't getting some of the same opportunities as the other interns.

Over time, I started speaking a little differently. But instead of my family and friends recognizing that I was trying to do better, learning other ways of speaking and living and growing, their message to me was: *Oh, so you go downtown and think you're too good. You come back talking white.*

I couldn't fault them for that, because that was how we grew up, that was what we were taught. I'd shed such thoughts, but I still understood the thinking. That somehow speaking more "properly" or grammatically, growing your vocabulary, going to some cultural event downtown, was somehow "putting on airs."

Beyond ignoring such limited thinking, I needed to attach myself to more supportive people—in Chicago as a kid, and now in D.C.

Matt was one of my supporters. He'd been chief of staff for John Boozman (R-Ark.) in his congressional and Senate offices for years and had also worked as a senior legislative assistant for Congressman Saxby Chambliss (R-Ga.). He knew D.C. well. "I think you can really do this," he told me. "I honestly think you're going to be successful."

Another guy, Michael, was proof of how support can come from unexpected places. Michael was a staff assistant for a congressional committee on Capitol Hill. We kept bumping into each other around town and eventually agreed to grab some lunch. During lunch, he said, "Give me your résumé. I might be able to help." I hid my smile. This guy was a staff assistant, much younger than me. He spent most of the day answering the phone and getting coffee for senior advisers, just like me. (To be fair, he actually got *paid* for it.) How was he going to help?

Three days later, I got a call from the Committee on House Administration saying the staff director wanted to meet with me. Turns out Michael was the son of Phil Kiko, a Capitol Hill veteran who'd filled numerous roles, including staff director for the Benghazi committee. Phil offered his help and mentorship and told me that I would be successful if I started my own firm. So did Todd, a lobbyist who'd introduced me around town when I first arrived. "I think you'll be successful," he said. "You're exactly the kind of guy who could actually pull this off."

All my networking was paying off.

While most people went out of their way to tell me that I *wasn't* going to be successful, that I *wouldn't* make it, that I needed to go back to Chicago, these few told me that they thought I'd do well. It was great to hear those kind words. Admittedly, I'd already made up my mind that I was going to step out and take on this new venture. I had faith in God and confidence in myself, and was fully convinced that I'd make it. I had to.

I started looking for business, scouring the network I'd built in Illinois. First, I tracked down all the legislators I'd ever lobbied on issues at the state level and asked if they'd feel comfortable making introductions for me. Most said no, but some agreed. I started meeting with companies and industries interested in doing business with me. Then they'd get my proposal, and I'd get another "no." Turns out most of them expected the new kid on the block to be supercheap, less than half what other consultants charged.

With every "no," I became more energized. More determined. Not necessarily to prove them wrong, but to prove to *myself* that I was right. That I *had* made the right decision.

Finally, I landed a job with a small community hospital in Chicago. It was on the brink of bankruptcy because it owed Medicare a big periodic interim payment and had less than twenty-four hours to come up with a million-plus dollars. If the hospital couldn't pay, the federal government would seize all of its incoming payments, and it'd be closed by the end of the month. This was a small safety-net hospital on the South Side, serving the black community. I worked all of my contacts on Capitol Hill and eventually got a hold of the senior legislative aide to Senator Dick Durbin (D-Ill.), the Senate Democratic whip.

"The community *needs* this hospital," I assured him. "And the hospital just needs more time to make it happen. They're ready and eager to renegotiate a deal to keep this valuable resource available." I laid out the new plan.

By the next day, Medicare had a change of heart. They restructured the payment plan, and that community hospital remained open.

It was an important victory—for my business and for my community back in Chicago. It felt like further proof I'd chosen the right path.

WASHINGTON, D.C., was such a big part of my journey, professionally and personally. In D.C., I was broke and hungry. I met and worked with some of the most powerful people in America. I made good friends from all age groups and backgrounds.

In the end, of course, it proved to be a good thing that I didn't find a job with a lobbying firm and had to create my own. The opportunities that came later were far better.

It *was* a tough journey, though, and I realize that some people don't have the endurance, or the faith, to continue in the face of such great resistance. But not a day goes by when I don't meet someone who's also put it all on the line and is working their butt off to achieve their professional and personal dreams. Many millennials, in particular, are willing to take a chance and do something outside the box, without the "right" degree or experience or any guarantee of future success. They're willing to start a business—a tech company, a nonprofit—with a couple of friends or alone in their apartment. They've rejected the narrative that most boomers lived by—that you should go to school, get a job, work for the same company for thirty years, trust that the company will take care of you after retirement with a pension and possibly stock options. They've rejected that narrative because it doesn't exist anymore in most cases. Most of the millennials who expect that path are, in my opinion, the ones still living at home. Getting angry at "the man" for keeping them down. Waiting for someone else, the government most likely, to come in and save the day. These are the ones who reject or don't take personal responsibility. Who get out of college, get their first job, and want to be the boss of the company the very same day. They're twenty-five, have no experience beyond that one semester as an intern, but they want that corner office and $100K in year one.

Facts: Unless you start a business yourself, it's incredibly unlikely you will be "the boss" immediately. Still, thanks to reality

TV and participation trophies, a lot of my generation feel otherwise. These are the angry ones. The lost ones. Those who, instead of digging deep, of figuring out another way, focus on the government taking care of them. That's why so many are willing to capitulate to the message of a Bernie Sanders or an Alexandria Ocasio-Cortez.

Still, every day, I meet millennials (and Gen Xers and Gen Zers) who are working hard, creating jobs, making their own way in the free market. Which makes infinite sense. Millennials pride themselves on being individuals. In most cases, we don't fit into the standards of our parents. We don't like to be told what to do. We'd like to create our own futures. Most of us are a bit more free-spirited and individualistic than our parents.

What more is conservatism than individual thought and freedom? The ability to have government stay out of our way and not tell us what to do. Not necessarily to have a boss, but to *be* the boss.

When Trump took office, regulations were slashed and taxes lowered. Within months, U.S. unemployment had dropped to its lowest level since 1969, more Americans were employed than ever before in our history, and job openings were at an all-time high and outnumbered job seekers. Unemployment rates for African Americans, Hispanics, Asian Americans, women, and young workers have reached the lowest levels in fifty-plus years. Blue-collar jobs have grown at the fastest rate in more than three decades.

The less government in our lives, the better we *all* do.

Certainly, we want to have safety nets to protect people and lift them up when needed. But we also absolutely want to make sure that they have the freedom to create the life that they desire for themselves.

Too many, it seems, are embracing a mindset of dependency. And, as someone who grew up in a dependency-oriented neighborhood *and* a dependency-oriented generation, I've already seen the future—and folly—imagined by millennials like Ocasio-Cortez. I grew up in a community that relied on the government for housing, food, security, schooling, income, and healthcare. Liberals like Sanders and Ocasio-Cortez *want* us to be dependent on government. Because they both believe that only they have the answers for how we should live and grow.

These lies and obstructions are keeping people from reaching their highest potential. This false notion that things are somehow unattainable or impossible to achieve because of an *external* source. This belief that the only help or solution will come from the government.

Pursuing your goals and striving for achievement can be difficult. As an individual, you *may* encounter more challenges than someone else—especially when coming from the countless handicaps of the inner city—but it is not impossible to achieve anything. I've seen firsthand how such thinking can ruin lives.

4

MURDER TO EXCELLENCE

THE TRUTH ABOUT INNER-CITY VIOLENCE— AND ITS SOLUTIONS

IT WAS LATE on Memorial Day. The night was surprisingly cool; it felt more like early spring than early summer. My younger brother was sitting in a parked car on the South Side of Chicago with a couple of his friends.

Two men approached, pulled automatic pistols, and started firing.

Bullets ripped through the car. Shattered windows. Punctured steel. And then skin. Later, the police would count twenty-five shell casings.

When my mother called me, all she could get out was "Your brother's . . ." and "There was a shooting. . . ." Too many anxious seconds passed before I could pull from her *which* of my brothers had been shot and whether he was alive. Throughout, I stood alone in my Washington, D.C., apartment, powerless and shaking with anger and sadness.

My brother had survived, I finally learned, and we thank God for that every day. But make no mistake, I could just as easily be discussing him in the past tense. My brother's best friend died in his arms that night. Shot through the back and into his heart. Both young men covered in blood: two more victims of the violence of Chicago.

There were four multiple-victim shootings in that same night. The holiday weekend left seven Chicagoans dead and another forty-five with gunshot wounds. The victims included a seventeen-year-old student and a twenty-year-old disabled man who'd been shot while at the park he visited every day. As far too many panicked relatives gathered outside Mount Sinai Hospital early Tuesday morning waiting for news of their loved ones, a passing car raced by and fired into the group. People were no longer safe even in a hospital parking lot.

No one was taken into custody for any of these shootings.

The number of shootings had, admittedly, dropped from the year before, when *seventy-one* people had been shot over the same weekend. At least that's how the local government was spinning it. Chief Fred Waller of the Bureau of Patrol, responsible for general field operations, including the protection of life and property, loudly proclaimed: "What I promise you is that we won't be defeated. I mean, I promise this city that we won't be defeated. We won't be overrun by that small group. That small element that's committing these restless acts. We will not . . . I promise you that we will not be defeated."

A "small element"? I couldn't believe what I was hearing.

The gun and gang violence rampant in Chicago that Memorial Day weekend wasn't some isolated burst of human slaughter. It had become, and remains today, a daily and piercing threat to everyone who lives in my hometown.

the root of these problems? Is it the influx of guns into the community? Is it the prohibition of drugs? Is it more police outfitted with more military-grade technology and weapons? All of the above? It seems that every side has an answer that just invites more questions.

The violence in the streets of Chicago is not an isolated problem.

Detroit, St. Louis, Memphis, Baltimore, Kansas City, Cleveland, Milwaukee, Oakland. . . . While these other cities across the nation might not match the headline-grabbing death tolls of my hometown, the causes of the violence and the plight of the citizens trapped within these economic deserts are the same.

This is a *national* crisis.

Our greatest cities have all the ingredients needed to create such violence: gangs, segregated communities, organized crime, budget-weakened security institutions, limited government capacity, ever-rising inequality, mass unemployment (one number, at least, newly slashed thanks to conservative deregulation). Some cities, like Chicago, just have it worse than others.

For too long, we've looked to our leaders for solutions, resources, and help. In this regard, both sides of the equation have failed.

AN EXAMPLE OF a failed leader from my hometown is Rahm Emanuel, Obama's former chief of staff and mayor of Chicago from 2011 to 2019. Throughout his reign, he proved nothing more than a failure, offering only promises, higher taxes, and "sanctuary" for everyone but the African Americans who were bleeding in his streets. I've said many times: Emanuel could not have cared less. Black lives didn't matter to him. Black *votes* mattered.

As mayor, he never *once* offered a sincere multipronged strategy to save his people from the architects of violence. He and the Democratic leadership across the state sought only to decrease gun violence via stronger gun laws, making Illinois's gun regulations some of the strictest in the nation. Those laws, of course, have proved largely ineffective in deterring or reducing gun violence. Someone should have warned Emanuel that criminals don't obey the law.

It's certainly true that Rahm Emanuel didn't pull the trigger that put bullets into my little brother's best friend. However, his half-hearted policies, inaction, and stubbornness enabled those who did, leaving American citizens to feel like they live in a war-torn country where a trip to the store for milk can cost a life.

It took far too long for the people of Chicago to grow impatient with Emanuel's inaction. Eventually, some got it. In August 2018, protesters shut down Lake Shore Drive to bring attention to the violence in the city.

I attended the protest, officially, as a Fox News reporter. Informally, I was there as a Chicagoan, as the brother of a victim of violence.

The people I met that day had plenty to say about Mayor Emanuel: That he was prioritizing illegal immigrants over Chicago residents. (Emanuel was one of the most vocal "sanctuary city" mayors.) That he really didn't care about the African American community; that he cared only about the elite within the city. That his focus was exclusively on getting reelected, when his job was to protect citizens and promote Chicago's economic health and stability. The frustration of those marching down Lake Shore Drive that day was deep and perceptible.

During these same protests, I ran into La Shawn Ford, a Democratic state representative whom I've known for many years. His solution to the violence started with an unlikely name: Donald Trump.

This senior Democrat told me—and anyone else who'd listen—that he *wanted* President Trump to come to Chicago, unlike Emanuel, who declared Chicago a "Trump-free zone." Ford also suggested that one of the temporary solutions would be to bring in the National Guard. For months, ever since Trump was elected, I'd been hearing that no Democrat would ever want to work with the new president. Until now.

I also became hopeful for my hometown when President Trump spoke out about Chicago. During the first weeks of his administration, he singled out Chicago as a city in desperate need of help, tweeting: "If Chicago doesn't fix the horrible 'carnage' going on, 228 shootings in 2017 with 42 killings (up 24% from 2016), I will send in the Feds!" Months later, he tweeted: "Seven people shot and killed yesterday in Chicago. What is going on there—totally out of control. Chicago needs help!" A year later, the president brought it up again at a graduation ceremony at the FBI Academy: "When you look at what's going on in Chicago. What the hell is going on in Chicago? What the hell is happening there? For the second year in a row, a person was shot in Chicago every three hours."

These callouts were encouraging signs for me. Finally, I thought, we had a leader who'd prioritize the crisis, a crisis that had already taken the lives of far too many. When considering the city leadership's failures, I believed—and still do—that

President Trump is a leader who can truly change the dynamic in my hometown. I'd love for him to order the U.S. attorney general and the FBI director to come up with a comprehensive plan to help solve this crisis.

While the long-term solutions will involve far more than increased police action, having the financial and martial support of the strongest nation on earth would certainly reset the stage. For months, however, all we'd heard from Chicago Democrats was that they didn't want President Trump in Chicago. Mayor Emanuel notoriously smirked on *The Late Show with Stephen Colbert* that Chicago was a "Trump-free zone" and that the city's motto was "A city he'll never sleep in. We don't want him." During the presidential primaries, liberal Chicago protesters stormed a Trump rally just hours before his appearance, forcing the campaign to cancel the event over security concerns. Trump was not allowed to come to Los Angeles, an American city. Outrageous. It told me a lot about the city's leaders. They'd chosen to try to solve a decades-old problem—one of their own making—by flying solo.

Which is why it's time to hold Democrats *completely* responsible for Chicago's violence. And this goes deeper than the inactivity or unwillingness to seek real help. For far too long, the street gangs and some Democrats have been in bed with one another, each scratching the other's back as Democratic politicians have sidled up to gang leaders for votes and community backing.

From the time of Prohibition until today, Chicago politicians have been known to placate and pay the gangs to employ their thugs as substitutes for political organizations—passing out leaflets, providing security. Gangs and politics have always gone hand in hand in the city. One gang lord, Jeff Fort of the El Rukns gang, took in $300,000 in city money in the 1980s to "cover costs of neighborhood programs." He'd earlier scored an invite to Richard Nixon's presidential inauguration. As recently as the 2010s, Chicago politicians routinely met with gang members at—according to an investigation by *Chicago* magazine—events "organized much like corporate-style job fairs," where the gang representatives "conducted hour-long interviews, one after the other, talking to as many as five candidates in a single evening."

The price to pay in Chicago politics? Maybe. Who but the gangs are expected to get anything done in these districts? Meanwhile, however, the left benefits, and the gangs' influence and arrogance grow.

As does the violence.

A WEEK AFTER my little brother was shot, I visited the White House for a meeting about an unrelated matter. Partway through the meeting, I took the opportunity to share my brother's story with the senior leadership and suggest that it was time for President Trump to back up his earlier tweets and do something meaningful for the people of Chicago. I detailed the shooting and the death of my brother's friend, to the staffers' surprise and horror. All of a sudden, these two men saw inner-city violence in a much different way. By speaking up, I'd made a statistic real. I was somebody they were familiar with, friends with, someone they'd seen on television, someone they knew personally.

Oftentimes, when we're talking about the White House or the hotshots at the state level, you have to wonder: Who do they *personally* know who's dealt with this issue? Few people, if any.

So many politicians and administrators on both sides of the aisle come from money and privilege, it can be difficult for them to understand. But when you can put a face on a situation, folk begin to look at an issue, any issue, differently.

After hearing my brother's story, the staffers asked me to assemble a group of Chicagoans who had different ideas on ways to curtail the violence. They even told me they'd be sharing our meeting and new plan with Jared Kushner, Trump's son-in-law and head of the new White House Office of American Innovation (a role invented for/by Kushner to "make recommendations to the President on policies and plans that improve government operations and services, improve the quality of life for Americans now and in the future, and spur job creation").

A week or two later—I suspect this was already scheduled, but maybe I'd helped move it along—the White House sent a small group of FBI and ATF agents to Chicago to help combat the violence. (One of those people ended up getting shot, if you can believe that!)

Meanwhile, I put my community group together—a combination of education, spiritual, and business leaders on the South Side. The discussion at least had begun. As with most serious problems, real solutions will take more time, and more real talk, and genuine effort. Everything is always easier said than done. But it's better than offering yet another round of simple solutions that haven't worked in decades.

WHEN IT COMES to gun violence, one of the great misconceptions is that hiring more police officers—or even bringing in the

National Guard—is going to fix everything. All too often, that's the *only* solution given: additional police.

Yet, the weekend my brother's friend was murdered, thirteen hundred extra officers had been deployed in addition to the normal patrols. And the year before, almost nine hundred extra officers had been working on Memorial Day weekend. The Chicago Police Department targeted areas where much of the city's violence occurs. They even parked a huge mobile command center on one of the city's most widely known open-air heroin markets (at Roosevelt Road and Independence Boulevard). Cops resorted to riding three or four to a squad car or going around in rented vans to accommodate all the extra officers on patrol.

And yet the shootings still happened.

To be clear, there are times when I've called for more police to come in. Sometimes that really is the first step. But *any* call I've made for sending in the National Guard has been for a short-term fix while other areas that have contributed to the hopelessness of the people and help to cause the violence (such as lack of income, public education, and so on) are addressed. No one wants to see tanks rolling down Michigan Avenue. More men with guns is only a temporary solution. In fact, adding more police without addressing the more fundamental issues first could even *increase* the violence.

All across the country, there are high levels of distrust between police and inner-city communities. And, in some cases, not all of this distrust is unearned. Following the riots in Ferguson, Missouri, in 2014 (sparked by the police shooting of Michael Brown, Jr.), a state investigation of the police department revealed that in a city of only 21,000 residents, *90,000* citations and summonses for municipal violations had been issued to its own citizens in the four years leading up to the riots. That's an average of nearly three citations a year for every household in the city.

When we pressure police departments across the country to prove that they've somehow both (a) reduced crime and (b) increased arrests at the same time—which, of course, would be impossible—there's bound to be some trouble. Serious crimes are overlooked or not written up (thus, "lower crime"), and minor offenses are often enforced to make it appear that the powers that be are hard at work. All for the sake of giving mayors and police commissioners something to brag about—a false narrative, one that's obvious to both the police and the inner city.

Chicago, too, has had a history of violence against its own people. From Jon Burge, a commander in the Chicago Police Department accused of torturing more than two hundred suspects in the 1970s and '80s in order to force confessions, to the shooting of Laquan McDonald, murdered in 2014 by a Chicago police officer who fired his entire magazine into the unarmed teen, the community has had reason to distrust the city's police force for years.

Still, it's imperative for the people of Chicago—and other cities across the country—to work with the police. Beyond the fact that most police officers are honorable and risking their lives to protect our rights, at this point it's a matter of self-preservation. The police *are* working to make our streets safer and routinely *do* hold their own to account when wrongdoing occurs.

We need to praise them for that, and not just attack the wrongs, because doing so opens up the opportunity for true community dialogue. Further, we've seen some use-of-force cases where the officers have been held accountable immediately and then fired. This, again, provides a chance for law enforcement to open up channels of communication and earn their community's trust. In this age of body cams and cellphones, there's far less opportunity for police corruption or abuse of power. These are positive developments.

A police organization I worked with in the past offers a class to young people and adults on how to interface and properly communicate with police. One thing they tell you is to follow the officer's instructions and not talk back. This advice was invaluable to me when I was growing up. People who decide to berate the police and not follow their directions are putting themselves in harm's way. White people *seem* to survive such encounters more often than people of color, an issue worth studying more closely and honestly. We clearly need to train officers in the same way we train soldiers when they're going into a foreign land. Considering that some of these officers come from the suburbs and have never truly interacted with African Americans before, they're missing a level of cultural understanding when they walk onto the job—one that could be the difference between pulling the trigger and not.

In our current situation, where the violence is so systemic, the two sides must listen to each other—*really* listen to each other. Coming up with ways to stop the violence *together* is a good strategy. Police and community leaders must regularly host community events and discuss the issues in the community, their actions, and possible solutions. The community, in turn, must confidentially give the police tips, especially since some people usually know who the perpetrators are. The days of "no snitching" must end. Communities have to start holding their own more accountable. For too long, there has been a culture of silence. You know there's gang activity going on, or you know who the shooter was, and you refuse to say anything. Before, when people kept quiet for fear of consequences, it affected only those in "the life." Now keeping quiet can get anyone killed. There needs to be a way for folk to anonymously report who's doing what and what's going on, without being subject to retaliation.

One citizen in Atlanta, the Reverend Markel Hutchins, began as an angry protester more than a decade ago when a ninety-two-year-old woman was shot to death by police during an unlawful raid for drugs at her home. (No drugs were found.) His first instinct was to address the police as the enemy. But within a few years, he was working directly *with* the police. Advocating *for* the police. Organizing citizen training throughout Atlanta and opportunities for the police and communities to communicate openly, to get to know each other better.

Hutchins is currently in the process of bringing his organization to Chicago. Good. We need it.

When I was growing up, police officers still walked through our neighborhood on foot, getting to know community members, building relationships. As a result, my grandparents and neighbors felt comfortable giving information to them. For the officers, it was hard to draw a weapon on a young friend with whom you'd recently talked about the Bulls.

ANOTHER MISCONCEPTION about gun violence is that if the government could only ban all guns in Chicago, everything would be fine. Chicago has the most comprehensive gun control laws in the country. Yet we still see a violent toll. Criminals, after all, don't much care for the law. Guns are bought and traded every day on the streets.

This is why, across America, the states with the strictest gun laws also have the biggest problems with gun-related fatalities. Honolulu, Chicago, San Francisco, Seattle, Portland (Oregon), D.C.: All have the most draconian gun laws on the books, yet they are *still* the cities where you're most likely to get shot. The only real change gun control has brought to these cities is that fewer law-abiding citizens have the ability to protect themselves from the criminals. Trust me, criminals think twice when they're not sure whether their target is carrying a gun.

One Chicagoan had to go all the way to the Supreme Court to secure the right to carry a weapon. Otis McDonald, a retired maintenance engineer, was almost eighty years old in 2008 when he sued the city over his constitutional right to own a pistol. (Chicago had issued a citywide ban on handguns in 1982, Bill of Rights be damned.) McDonald described his neighborhood as having been taken over by gangs and drug dealers. All he wanted was access to the same weapons they had. Democratic leaders in Chicago and Illinois fought him every step of the way, saying that he had no such right. McDonald eventually took his case all the way to the U.S. Supreme Court, which ruled in his favor by a 5–4 vote in 2010. (Good thing there were five Second Amendment–abiding conservatives on the bench.)

The ruling in *McDonald v. City of Chicago* changed the landscape across the country. It meant that cities could no longer overregulate people's use of guns or prevent them from having them. Here was a citizen who really took the bull by the horns and said, "Hey, I'm not going to take it." And that made a difference. (My little brother is, and was, a legal gun owner. He says he wishes he'd had his gun on that fateful night, to better protect his best friend.)

Neither putting more cops on the street nor fixing our gun laws by making them less restrictive is a long-term solution to gun violence. In fact, there's no *one* right answer when it comes to solving the larger crisis. It'll need to be done with a multi-pronged attack.

The first matter is that we need information. All too often, policy issues and decisions are being made with decades-old data and assumptions.

Of the top thirty causes of death in the United States, gun violence is the least researched. According to a study published in the *Journal of the American Medical Association,* gun violence should have received almost $1.5 *billion* in federal research money between 2004 and 2015, but instead it received only $22 *million.* We know far less about gun violence than we do about almost every other medical issue. As a result of this lack of research, policy makers remain ignorant about many aspects of gun violence, including the most effective ways to reduce it. There are thousands of studies waiting to be performed, but the money to complete them hasn't been allocated. Because of this, more than one hundred medical organizations have beseeched Congress to restore full funding for this research.

Political leaders and police must also get out into the streets and speak to both those affected by the violence and those committing it. Chicago, like many large cities in America, is a highly segregated city. Racial and ethnic groups tend to live in their own areas. It's far too easy to forget about people in other areas and other groups. This is one reason there's an abundance of resources going into communities other than the inner city, especially when people in those areas are more vocal and active in government. (Not to say that African Americans in Chicago haven't been vocal and active, because we've been protesting for decades.)

As a special correspondent for Fox News, I've had the privilege of returning to inner-city neighborhoods to hear what residents think about gun violence. I've visited the most impoverished and dangerous neighborhoods in Chicago: Austin, Pullman, Washington Park, and the notorious Englewood. (In spans of just three months, police often record five hundred or more violent incidents and about a dozen murders in Englewood alone. Englewood is *three square miles;* there are *countries* with lower crime numbers.)

On these reporting trips to the communities where I grew up, I've interviewed law-abiding citizens alongside younger gang members, as well as the same ones who used to threaten me and who still perpetrate violence to this day. I wanted to get the gang members' point of view and understand why they do it. Those on the block seem to understand the issue. "Everybody just wants to do better," one woman said. "Wants to rock the better jeans, the better shoes. To have something of their own. So these boys, with few other options, think, *Hey, let me sell drugs to get it.* The hope is that if you get some of these teens into jobs, get some legally earned money in their pocket, maybe they'll stop."

The gangbangers agree. "No jobs out here," they told me. "People do what they need to do to survive. They're gonna rob, sell drugs, do whatever to survive. . . . That's the life."

I have met numerous young men who *want* to change but don't have access to legit entry-level jobs and don't see a path to a legit life. The numbers back this up. In 2016, it was reported that 47 percent of African American men between the ages of twenty and twenty-four in Chicago were unemployed or out of school. Much of the city has only a shadow economy to rely on. There are no real business opportunities that folk are aware of—or, if there are, they don't qualify for the jobs or can't pass a background check. Still, when asked if they would leave the gang life if I could guarantee they could find a legitimate job, almost all of them said yes.

But getting a job is only the start. *Keeping* it is where the real work begins. Showing up on time; showing up at all. Taking orders from someone who's not threatening you or handing you a hundred for walking a bag across town. Taking orders from anyone is often seen as being weak. These young people need to learn how to go to work. Too many are married to the gang life because they've never been exposed to anything else.

This is why it's so important that we go into the schools. To make sure there are classes and programs, ways to incentivize youth with jobs that aren't just for the summer but year-round. To reverse the false notions that speaking proper English is "talking white" or that getting good grades and caring about school is only for "lames" or "dorks."

While still living in Chicago, I wanted to do some volunteering and mentoring in this regard. To expose as many kids as I could to the same work ethic I'd learned from my grandfather and from those I'd met at the alderman's office and Social Security Administration. I eventually came upon Phillip Jackson and The Black Star Project. Jackson, who'd previously worked as chief of staff for both Chicago Public Schools and the CEO of the Chicago Housing Authority, designed Black Star to help students realize their educational and life potential.

I began speaking at local schools at Phillip's invitation. The idea was to show these kids another path. That there were people from the South Side who'd grown up and made it without joining a gang. That earning a paycheck gave you a wonderful feeling. That building a résumé was a long and productive endeavor. That faith in God could be a tangible experience.

I'd tell them my story, admit to spending the bulk of my childhood staying in my room and watching the news on TV, working for the alderman, making my way to positions with the state and federal governments. In these marginalized areas, they'd met few people who'd done such things. Further, it was important for them to understand that even if they'd made mistakes early in life, they still had an opportunity to course-correct and make something of themselves.

Another person I met while reporting for Fox News in Chicago was Tyrone Muhammad, who runs a program called Ex-Cons for Community and Social Change. He spent about thirty years in prison. When he got out, he started this program, which employs ex-cons to go back into the communities where they sold drugs or stole from their neighbors, the communities they brought bloodshed to. They talk to youth, young gangbangers like they once were, helping to get them employed in legitimate jobs. These are stories that we normally don't hear. They are about effecting change at a real-world level and can help change the narrative.

Muhammad told me, "We're men who recognize we made a mistake. We're not sitting around now waiting on the politicians, the legislations, to change our condition. We know that we helped perpetrate some of the violence in our community . . . and learned we will have to change it ourselves." These communities need men who are willing to stand in the gap like that. To show teens: *This is how you legally earn an income. These are the mistakes we made. This is what you want to do and what you want to avoid.*

There are hundreds of such programs—nonprofits and foundations—available in cities across the United States, helping to fight violence. The biggest problem is that most of them are underfunded, and few people in the community even know they exist. Simply making the community aware of the programs already in place could have an immediate and lasting impact.

MANY OF CHICAGO'S neighborhoods are pockmarked with vast swaths of empty land. These are the spaces where schools, job training centers, stores, and other businesses offering opportunities for aboveboard employment should be.

Alas, the entrenched Democratic leadership has not yet invited businesses to come back, not yet provided the proper incentives and tools to rebuild these communities. It's the old liberal story: overtaxation and overregulation. The industries and other businesses left. The tax base vanished. The economy in these neighborhoods became desolate.

An illegal economy filled the void.

But it's a catch-22. Major businesses and high-wage jobs won't come back to Englewood until it's safe to do so. And it won't be safe, largely, until the legit jobs and money come back. It's hard to get businesses to come in, even with tax incentives, when they fear for their employees' lives.

The biggest problem, perhaps, is that there is a deficit in personal responsibility. It is in this area that conservative values—like respect for parents, authority, and human life—can make the biggest difference. Yet far too many parents believe that their own parents were too hard on them when they were growing up. So they now allow their kids to do as they please. No limitations, no boundaries. And those kids often become adults way too soon. Living like there's no tomorrow. Not valuing human life.

And the result is the bloodshed.

There are also not enough fathers in the home. More than 75 percent of African Americans are born out of wedlock. That's—yell at me if you want—an issue. Family structure is in shambles. "Tragic" is not a strong enough word. Young people often head to the street corners seeking guidance because that's where their peers are and they don't have a father at home. Peers weren't meant to raise one another. And while some of the best men I know were raised by women, there's no substitute for a male role model in a young man's life.

That's a point that needs to be made and defended without contrition for making it. Black males are at the greatest risk of dropping out of school, of going to prison, of being killed. They need the support of men who know what it means to be a man and understand the specific struggles associated with being a man. Especially a young black man.

We need more mentoring in the city of Chicago. There needs to be an acceptance of personal responsibility, because we can't rely on the government to solve all our problems. And that includes the violence.

My heart aches for those, including the family of my little brother's best friend, who've experienced the unbearable pain of inner-city violence.

Shortly after the shooting, my brother moved away from Chicago. I don't blame him. Chicago, like too many once great

American cities, is plagued by a culture of death. There's an expectation each year that when the temperature reaches a certain level and people start spending more time outside, blood will spill in the streets. Such thinking is unacceptable.

I'm not naïve. I realize it's impossible to completely end killings in Chicago. But cutting the death toll substantially is an achievable goal.

In 2011, Kanye West (yeah, yeah, Kanye again; what can I say?) released a song titled "Murder to Excellence," in which he details the sad state of affairs involving black-on-black murders in Chicago and asks: "Is it genocide?"

City kids are often the most creative, resourceful, inventive, and organized young people you'll ever meet. Their survival frequently depends on these traits. Without action against violence, we risk losing important members of what could—and should—be one of the greatest generations in human history. These young Americans have been so marginalized by conditions in their neighborhoods that they will never realize their full potential. Too often, the most promising talent can be found in the graveyard.

What might those three thousand shootings in 2017 have accomplished? What businesses could they have built? What art created? Justice delivered? If you don't think such magnificence is possible, then we are not yet on the same page. As a true conservative, I believe that there is a greatness in each of us. That the pursuit of happiness is a God-given right for all. First, though, we clearly need to protect life.

The hand-wringing and inertia of the Democratic leaders in Chicago put those young lives at risk every day. Now that there's new leadership in my hometown, I encourage them to do two things not yet tried.

First, they should gather experts from across the country— from across the *world*—with proven programs of violence prevention on their résumés, not those who only want to line their pockets with much-needed community money.

Second, they should reach out to the "other side"—to *any* side with an idea or the funds to help. President Obama never truly extended a hand to Chicago (his adopted hometown), never provided any substantial federal resources. We now have a leader in Washington who's willing to work with Chicago. The White House could—and would, I believe—fully fund programs aimed at providing positive alternatives to at-risk individuals before they fall into patterns of violence. If President Trump is serious about helping the people of Chicago, and I believe he is, the city can't turn his help away.

A "Trump-free zone"? Chicago has become a boneyard, my friends. The posturing and politics must end.

For when an "enemy" becomes an ally, that's often the best time to make real and lasting change.

5

"BRUH, YOU'RE FROM EVANSTON"

TEAMING UP WITH THE "OTHER SIDE"

FOR MONTHS, I was out to get Richard Fowler.

Richard is a media personality and analyst. Like me, he's also young and black and on Fox News. But unlike me, he's a liberal, and he'd been on the network for years before I got there. I knew, however, that it was only a matter of time before we crossed paths.

The first day we were scheduled to debate some issue together on camera, I walked up to introduce myself. I didn't care that he was a Democrat. He was a colleague in the media and another guy working hard at his career. "Just wanted to say hello," I said, shaking his hand. "Looking forward to being on air with you."

He looked bored. Dismissive. Right away, he struck me as . . . well, as if he thought I was beneath him. Maybe, I figured, he was just annoyed Fox News had brought on another young guest to debate. Fair enough.

"Where are you from?" I asked, hoping to break the ice.

"Chicago," he said.

"Really?" Cool, I thought. Maybe that could bridge this gap between us. "Which part?" I asked.

"Evanston," he said.

Evanston is a suburb twenty miles outside of Chicago.

I might have laughed.

"That isn't Chicago," I said.

"Fuck you," he said, and walked away to the makeup room.

Okay, maybe I shouldn't have dissed Evanston, but I'm not sure his response was necessary either. It got worse on set. Richard was notorious for running over people on air, just barreling over them, but some of his data was questionable, so at several points I stopped his monologue and challenged him on it. "What facts do you have to back that up?" I kept saying.

Eventually, he snapped. "I got them from the newspaper. Do you even read those?"

Ouch. After that, it was gloves off. Every time we went on air, I was gunning for him, and vice versa. It was, I admit, personal. It also made for good TV, so the network loved it and kept inviting us to appear together. Months into this relationship, he eventually called me to offer a truce. "Listen," he said, "we're the only two young black men on the network. Let's not do this black-on-black crime on air anymore. Let's call a truce and move on."

I agreed. Weeks later, we were back on air together. I let him talk before saying my piece. Then he did it again. Broke all the rules. Talked over me, interrupted me, hogged the whole "conversation," and basically ran out the clock while saying I didn't know what I was talking about.

I was ten feet off the set when someone said, "Gianno, you have a call."

It was a producer from another show. "I just saw you," he said. "That was brutal. Don't let Richard do that to you again."

I tracked down Richard a minute later. "I thought we made a deal to be respectful and let each other get our points across?"

He just laughed. "You know how it is, Gianno. Ha, ha."

"You know I got you next time," I warned.

The next few times we were on together, I kept baiting him. "Richard doesn't know what he's talking about," I'd say, trying to get a reaction. Nothing.

One day, Fox News host Ed Henry and I were having lunch together. He told me he was hosting *Fox & Friends Weekend* and invited me to come on. I didn't know what the topic would be until the morning of the show. Turns out we would be discussing the violence in Chicago. I was really looking forward to having that discussion.

I was waiting in the greenroom when someone popped their head in.

"Is Richard here yet?" they asked.

"Um . . . Richard . . . who?" I asked.

It was Fowler, of course. He was going to be on with me. For about ten seconds, I was annoyed, then I realized that the opportunity I'd been waiting months for had finally arrived. The day's topic was Chicago, specifically. I had him. As we walked down the hall toward the studio, I'd already started producing the entire segment in my head. This time, I knew, Richard would take the bait.

The segment began. After arguing for a bit, I tossed out my lure. "Unlike Richard," I said, "I didn't *read* about the news in Chicago. I lived it."

Richard couldn't resist. He stepped right into it. "What the home audience doesn't know is that I'm from Chicago. I work in Chicago. . . . And if you talk with the people in Chicago—"

"Bruh . . ." I called him out, continuing despite his rambling. "Bruh, you're from *Evanston,* Richard. In order for you to know what the weather's like in Chicago, you'd have to read the newspaper. You're not from Chicago, bruh. You don't know the environment, you didn't live there."

Richard's face collapsed on national television.

By the time I stepped out of the studio, I'd already been hit with an avalanche of tweets and texts. "You got him!" "Too many bruhs for me." "Hilarious!" "312!"

Meanwhile, Fox News didn't post the segment on its website that day or put it out on Twitter. I finally realized I'd said "bruh" about six too many times and figured they'd never invite me back. Still, the *Washington Examiner*—which I was writing for at the time—pulled some strings and got the clip so I could put it on my personal Facebook page that Monday.

By Tuesday, it was everywhere. The clip was being passed all over Chicago and then nationally, making it onto large urban platforms like The Shade Room, one of urban America's most followed websites. The TSA agent at the airport was yelling "Bruh!" at me. People all over the country were talking about it. Someone even made a rap mixtape with my face on it, titled "Bruh, You're from Evanston." The local press jumped all over the debate about whether Evanston should be considered part of Chicago or not. A local politician from Evanston adopted the slogan "Bruh, I'm from Evanston," and he ended up being elected mayor.

When the segment went viral, I texted Richard: *You good, bro?* He came back with: *Hey, I'm good.*

Still, I kind of felt bad for him. Everybody and their mama was making fun of him. I'd been looking to take him down a peg, sure, but this "victory" felt as hollow as it should have. It's not why I'd gotten involved in politics *or* television. We'd been talking about very serious issues in Chicago, issues of life and death. And I'd used my position and opportunity selfishly, carelessly.

I called my trusted ally and peer mentor, Eboni K. Williams, at the time a colleague at Fox News, who's like a sister to me.

"Hey," I said. "This thing with Richard has gone crazy viral. There's got to be something we can do for the people of Chicago." My thought was that we could speak at local schools about our unique journeys into the media and how we'd grown personally to reach that point. I wanted to provide role models for the youth of Chicago, hopefully to inspire those in despair. And we obviously *had* to include Richard. We called him, and I said, "Richard, uh, this is me and Eboni on."

"Okay, great," he said. He didn't seem happy to hear from me. Understandably so.

But I kept going. "Listen," I said. "We had this moment. It's become a very big thing for a bit. So let's do something with it. Let's meet in Chicago—you, me, and Eboni—and go speak to the youth. About guns, gangs, schooling, mentors. You know? We both know the town in our way. The three of us could really do something impactful. Let's do this."

Richard was silent.

"Richard?" I prompted.

"Okay," he said. "Let's do it."

I called a number of schools to set up meetings for talks. Some were receptive, while others quickly said no thanks when they heard "Fox News." One principal said she was all in, but the day before we were scheduled to appear, she called me. "We can't do it," she told me. "We've got to cancel. The parent-teacher board doesn't like the fact that you guys appear on Fox News. They don't like Republicans. So we can't do it. I'm sorry."

That was shocking to me. Our talk could literally change lives. I was disappointed that this school would miss the opportunity to hear from us due to the Fox News and Republican connection.

Still, we had four events scheduled over the course of two days. Out of our own pockets, we paid for our airfare, hotel, and car rental. We visited some of the most poverty-stricken areas in the city, where the schools needed the most attention. Most of the students were already familiar with the clip of Richard and me from *Fox & Friends Weekend,* but they weren't privy to the backstories of how we had ended up in front of the camera. The sight of three young, black, successful TV professionals, well dressed and articulate, but also able to speak in familiar cultural colloquialisms, proved a shock for many. To see that we—not rappers, athletes, or drug dealers—had made it out of the hood was eye-opening for these young people.

One of our events was at Emil G. Hirsch Metropolitan High School, just several blocks from the first house my family lived in after my grandmother's home was foreclosed on. The things the school officials shared with us about the student population were heartbreaking—even for me, a guy who'd come up in that community. Stories of recent student murders near the school, the fear students experienced walking through numerous gang territories to get to school, the daily anxiety of perhaps dying while simply trying to get an education. They brought the entire student body into the auditorium to hear us speak. One student we met had a girlfriend and child with whom he lived, and the girl's mother told him he *had* to go to school every morning and he *had* to take the child with him. Every day, this student brought his child to school, and an administrator took care of the baby while he went to class.

Looking these young people in the eye and telling them about my background—the fact that I understood what it felt like to grow up in extreme poverty right down the street from their high school—and seeing myself as a kid in them had a big impact on me. When I told them that, like some of their parents, my mother had been addicted to crack cocaine, you could see the shock on their faces. After the event, several students came up to tell us *their* stories, to exchange email addresses with us, and to take photos.

After speaking at the four schools, I toured Chicago's hardest-hit areas with Eboni, giving her a firsthand view of a city we speak so much about on air. We recorded footage for my Instagram page that got picked up by the national media. Vacant lots and boarded-up houses. Drug deals and gang activity. It remained the way of life for the people living here.

That week, we also did a press tour with local and national media, which we hoped would encourage others to find their own ways to make a difference.

Here's my point in sharing this story: Far too often, we demonize the other side and forget that they're usually trying to solve the same problems we are . . . just in different ways. That's true whether it's your old college friends on Facebook (*I'll block any supporter of X!*) or all those people drawn to the promise of what *could* get done on Capitol Hill.

It didn't take much for Richard and me to bury the hatchet and discuss our differences in a way that might do some good. Bipartisan politics on a small scale. But anything that works on a small scale can also work on a larger scale at the highest government and other levels in the land.

I will never forget the feeling of joining together with two people I respect for the betterment of the city. It was a blessing of the greatest proportions. We had an opportunity to turn a fun viral moment into something truly meaningful.

And you will be happy to know that Richard and I are now pals.

I FIRST ENCOUNTERED this kind of unlikely teamwork when I started working at the Illinois State Capitol. I lobbied the legislature, government officials, and consultants of all stripes and both parties. It was there that, for the first time, I began to be accepted by black people as a Republican.

Malcolm Weems, a ranking Democrat and a respected chief of staff for the governor's budget office, was one of the first black senior bureaucrats who took me seriously. He pulled me aside shortly after I arrived in Springfield. "Listen," he said. "I know you're a Republican, but at the end of the day, you're one of us. You actually care about the black community. I know because of what others have said and what I have observed. We got you."

He didn't care one iota that I was a Republican. Rather, he saw it as an advantage, because I'd become the black community's representative in the GOP. It was exactly the kind of opportunity I'd been hoping for. Weems and others understood that I had a voice inside the other team and could maybe help people on both sides see things differently. He understood that we might do some good together. It was great to have someone like him advocate for me.

If you're thinking *I see how it is; you guys have this little club together* . . . well, you're right. Only 12 percent of the country is African American. We know that to get anything done, you sometimes need to sit down with the "enemy" and sort things out. The fact that nearly 40 percent of prison inmates are black men and that 40 percent of black children live in poverty only makes bipartisan efforts all the more important.

Such camaraderie continued when I arrived in D.C. I quickly learned that people on both sides of the aisle were working to cut deals and sometimes to help our bosses see the bigger picture and put politics and posturing aside. Bipartisanship is rare in D.C., but it does exist.

The bigger picture, it may surprise you, is actually remarkably clear.

Here are some specific plank points and goals declared at the national party convention in 2016:

- Raising workers' wages and supporting working families
- Protecting workers' fundamental rights
- Expanding access to affordable housing and homeownership
- Building twenty-first-century infrastructure
- Fostering/returning U.S. manufacturing
- Promoting innovation and entrepreneurship
- Supporting America's small businesses
- Creating jobs for America's young people
- Reforming our criminal justice system
- Fixing our broken immigration system
- Investing in rural America
- Providing quality and affordable education

- Reducing prescription drug costs
- Combating drug and alcohol addiction
- Promoting public health
- Ending violence against women
- Preventing gun violence
- Supporting a strong military
- Confronting global threats
- Being a world leader

I'm sure you'll notice I didn't say *which* party convention. That's because these goals were touted as primary objectives at both the Democratic National Convention in Philadelphia and the Republican National Convention in Cleveland.

While we clearly disagree over how best to solve these problems—bigger government versus personal responsibility and self-determination—the desire to address these issues is indistinguishable.

Surely, partisan hostilities can be set aside for discussion, compromise, and tangible progress for the American people.

It *has* happened in recent memory.

During the Obama years, it took genuine bipartisan efforts to craft important free trade deals with South Korea, Panama, and Colombia; the Violence Against Women Reauthorization Act of 2013; the Every Student Succeeds Act (No Child Left Behind 2.0); and the Medicare Access and CHIP Reauthorization Act of 2015.

But, undeniably, it's been a while.

In Arizona senator John McCain's last official address to the Senate, though voting *against* the GOP's half-hearted effort to repeal Obamacare, he specifically emphasized the need for bipartisanship and called upon "the necessity of compromise in order to make incremental progress on solving America's problems." McCain said: "I hope we can again rely on humility, on our need to cooperate, on our dependence on each other to learn how to trust each other again and by so doing better serve the people who elected us.... Let's trust each other. Let's return to regular order. We've been spinning our wheels on too many important issues because we keep trying to find a way to win without help from across the aisle."

I felt the same frustration.

For months, I'd pretended to wonder why the Democratic Party, which receives such enormous support from African Americans, wasn't more supportive of the criminal justice reform bill the White House was working on.

The answer, of course, was Trump.

This was the most comprehensive criminal justice reform bill in recent history—what would become the First Step Act. The measure was introduced in the Senate on November 15, 2018, by Senate Judiciary Committee chairman Charles E. Grassley (R-Iowa) and minority whip Richard J. Durbin (D-Ill.), among others. Intended to be a true bipartisan effort, this bill was also supported by groups such as the American Civil Liberties Union, the Fraternal Order of Police, the Koch brothers, and many evangelical Christian groups.

The goal for all was to reduce mandatory sentences for some drug-related felonies, make more low-level offenders eligible for early release, and provide more funding for anti-recidivism programs. If passed, the bill would reduce thousands of prison sentences, primarily in the African American community, and save the federal government millions of dollars in the process.

You'd think Democrats would have come running to the White House for an opportunity to work with the administration on this bill. Fat chance. Instead, several high-profile Democrats soundly rejected the proposed legislation, from former attorney general Eric Holder to a coalition of leading Senate Democrats, including Cory Booker of New Jersey and Kamala Harris of California. (Funny how many of these saboteurs would soon run for president.) In a joint letter, these senators claimed that the measure would be "a step backwards" and that prison reform would fail if Congress did not simultaneously completely overhaul the nation's sentencing laws. Also signing the letter were Representative Sheila Jackson Lee of Texas and Representative John Lewis of Georgia, the civil rights icon. More telling, Dick Durbin, the guy who'd originally sponsored the bill, now had a change of heart.

All this posturing once again proved the hypocrisy of the Democratic Party. Instead of working with the administration on a significant piece of legislation for the black community—which they *claimed* to represent—they instead obstructed and disingenuously asserted that it didn't go far enough.

To be fair, some vocal Democrats were brave enough to challenge their party's resistance to the bill. Congressman Hakeem Jeffries of New York scolded his party for what he called the "all-or-nothing approach" of the bill's opponents. Jeffries warned his colleagues that they risked losing focus on the people who would most stand to benefit from even limited congressional action. "There are thousands of people who are incarcerated right now who will be helped immediately if the First Step Act becomes law," Jeffries said. "They don't care about politics. They need the help, and they need the help now." And well-known former Obama administration official Van Jones tweeted: "Give the man his due: @realDonaldTrump is on his way to becoming the uniter-in-Chief on an issue that has divided America for generations."

Both Jones and Jeffries are African American. But denying Trump a victory clearly superseded common sense and the desire to serve their most loyal constituents. With so much on the line, both parties—especially the Democrats—needed to work with the administration to get this legislation passed and turn the tide of American justice. Meanwhile, the people who could truly benefit from the legislation remained in prison.

Even more damning for Democrats was that they had been the ones who'd made the epic error of supporting and pushing through Bill Clinton's 1994 crime bill. That bill—which I like to call the "modern-day slavery bill"—led directly and rapidly to the overcriminalization of African Americans throughout the country. For petty crimes like smoking or selling insignificant amounts of weed—crimes that some states have eliminated altogether and many local governments now give minor fines for, almost like a parking ticket. Thanks to Clinton's bill (and, previously, Reagan's "war on drugs"), the grim reality is that, statistically, almost every black person in America has had some interaction with the criminal justice system—either personally or through a family member.

Worst of all was when Clinton later praised the "successes" of the crime bill. During a 2016 presidential campaign event for his wife, Hillary, he claimed, "Because of that bill, we had a 25-year low in crime, a 33-year low in the murder rate." The event and his speech were soon interrupted by a Black Lives Matter group—and for good reason. Independent analysis has found that the bill had a "modest" effect on crime rates, at best. Democrats often claim they gave the black community the 1994 crime bill because "they asked for it," when, in fact, Jesse Jackson, the most prominent leader of the black community at that time, spoke before Congress warning of the dangers of the bill. In the end, the Democrats passed the bill with the majority of the Republicans voting *against* it.

By 2014, African Americans constituted 2.3 million, or 37 percent, of the 6.8 million Americans who were incarcerated. Since the United States has the largest corrections population in the world, this literally translates to African Americans being the most incarcerated group of people on earth. A very sad reality. And sad for me personally, considering I have close family members who've been, shall we say, "impacted" by this legislation. I am not alone, of course. Millions of others in the black community can say the same.

I saw the First Step Act as a clear opportunity to right this wrong, but the left did not want to see the legislation succeed, and the press hardly covered the issue or the possibility that the bill might pass. It became obvious that many Democrats would rather see black people stay in jail than give President Trump any credit for supporting this significant legislation. (It didn't help, I suspect, that Trump's son-in-law, Jared Kushner, was a major force behind the push to pass it.)

While we waited for something *both* parties had claimed to want *before* Trump's election to become law, the U.S. Sentencing Commission estimated that roughly 2,250 inmates per year would have their sentences reduced under the new legislation. And an additional 3,000 inmates could serve shorter sentences under the retroactive application of the 2010 Fair Sentencing Act. Both bills addressed mostly low-level offenses. If the First Step Act passed, judges would have greater flexibility in sentencing versus being forced to implement the mandatory minimum sentences required by Clinton's 1994 law. Although the legislation applied only to federal prisons, the bill would likely inspire, according to many studies, legislation that would impact local prison populations as well.

The GOP was in a perfect position to set things back in the right direction. During the summer of 2018, however, everything flip-flopped.

Senate majority leader Mitch McConnell (R-Ky.) was suddenly *not* committed to bringing the First Step Act to the floor. I'd been told by sources on the Hill that McConnell felt the bill was causing too many intra-caucus squabbles and was no longer "worth" the potential political fallout. He was worried that those like Senator Tom Cotton (R-Ark.), who'd led a misinformation campaign for months in an effort to kill the bill, would make statements alleging that it would allow hardened career criminals out of jail, completely ignoring the safety valves and language of the actual bill. In August, Cotton went so far as to write an op-ed full of such assertions.

His scare tactics were beginning to work until Senator Mike Lee (R-Utah) stepped in with his own op-ed rebutting each one of Cotton's assertions, calling them untrue and intellectually dishonest. Lee opined, "As a former federal prosecutor, I am clear-eyed about crime. I have nothing but respect for law-enforcement officials, who put themselves in danger every single day in order to protect the public. I know from experience that dangerous criminals exist—individuals who are incapable of or uninterested in rehabilitation and change. We should throw the book at those people. But my time as a prosecutor also tells me that not every criminal is dangerous or incapable of living a productive life. My faith as a Christian teaches me that many people are capable of redemption. And my instincts as a conservative make me believe that the government can be reformed to work better. For those reasons, I believe the First Step Act is legislation that deserves the support of all conservatives."

Even so, Cotton's original op-ed proved effective enough that some important Republican senators—including Marco Rubio of Florida and Ted Cruz of Texas—wavered in their support. The Democratic leadership smelled blood in the water. Figuring that McConnell was stuck, they tried once again to prove to the American people—specifically African Americans—how racist the GOP was. *See, the Republicans don't want you out of jail!* they said. And then, in what I have to admit was a smart pivot, the Democrats switched course. Now, ironically, they were *backing* the act with minor changes attached.

People's lives were being used as a political football. But it was all theater. The majority of the Republicans in the Senate were, by my count, still in favor of the bill. I had been working on criminal justice issues for years, leading meetings in conjunction with National Bar Association then-president Ben Crump with the chairmen of the House and Senate Judiciary Committees on other criminal justice reforms. In this case, we just had some work to do to convince people to set aside their political egos for the greater good.

IN LATE NOVEMBER 2018, I traveled to D.C. to lobby one of the most important measures of my lifetime. I wasn't alone. For months, I'd been advocating for the bill on TV and keeping my ear to the ground on Capitol Hill. Conservative firebrand Candace Owens knew about my advocacy for the First Step Act and asked me to join other conservative voices in D.C. to put on a demonstration of democracy in action. Owens is a far-right commentator and political activist. Her career has been controversial, as her rhetoric is often intentionally confrontational and incendiary.

After speaking with Candace, I booked my ticket and hotel and got ready to leave Los Angeles that night. Wanting to lobby this legislation the right way, I reached out to Mitch McConnell's and Chuck Grassley's respective committee counsel to discuss the status of the legislation and see which committee members should be targeted to ensure success. The majority of GOP members were fully in favor of the bill, but I knew our group needed the right strategy to push McConnell to bring this legislation to the floor.

We then walked the halls using the list of members I'd compiled. For us this wasn't "simply" lobbying a good bill. This was personal. This was a major opportunity specifically for the black community.

One person we definitely needed to visit was Senator Cruz. Like Senator Cotton, he'd been muddying the waters and causing confusion. We soon learned a lot more than what the media was reporting. His criticism of the bill, like Cotton's, didn't hold up under scrutiny. We demanded a meeting with Cruz, and when we got it, we pressed him. The senator told us he felt the bill could result in the release of dangerous criminals, even though, as he well knew, federal inmates would first have to go through vigorous analysis put in place by the Department of Justice and their own local wardens. Ultimately, it became clear that Cruz didn't trust the wardens or the DOJ on this matter, although he couldn't provide any data to support his claim.

I asked Cruz if he would at least ask McConnell to send the

bill to the floor. He said no. Unless the Senate was willing to support Cruz's amendment to the bill—an amendment that none of us had seen but that Cruz claimed would help prevent violent criminals from being released—he said that McConnell would not bring the bill to the floor.

I told the senator he was effectively standing in the way of criminal justice reform. "Your way," I challenged him, "or no way at all?"

He denied that claim, but it appeared to me and the rest of us who'd come to Washington that day that was exactly what was going on. Politicians are self-interested. The bigger the issue, the bigger the stage, the more self-interest comes into it. And the more game playing.

I was on a plane to L.A. when I got a message from a friend, a senior official at the White House who'd been one of the early architects of the bill. "I heard you were in town whooping up some votes for my bill," he said.

I told him I was legitimately hopeful that we were going to get this done and then promised to keep up the pressure on Democrats *and* Republicans during my appearances on Fox News.

The next day, a piece about our group's visit appeared online. I started getting calls and texts from many of my Hollywood celebrity friends. Big names. People with millions of social media followers. People with big brand deals.

But they weren't sending me words of praise and thanks for supporting legislation that would help the black community.

"What are you doing?" they asked.

I was confused.

"You're working with Candace Owens? Are you serious?" they said. "You got to think about your brand and reputation, doing any work with her."

My brand and reputation? Rest assured, I was aware of my "brand" and the minor blowback I might get long before I headed to D.C.

"Are you joking right now?" I shouted back into the phone. "This bill is *for* black people. For the community! Are *you* being serious?"

Owens is all in with Trump and sometimes says things I don't agree with. But none of that mattered to me in this case. From what I could tell, she was very serious and passionate about this issue for all the right reasons. Why wouldn't I want to work with her, or anyone else, on this?

About a month after our visit, Congress passed the First Step Act, and it was signed into law by President Trump.

Those folk on the phone didn't care about my reasons for supporting the bill. Not really. Many of the naysayers would rather have seen black Americans stay in jail if it meant Trump succeeding. And this is exactly what the Democratic Party wants. They don't want *any* conservative being seen as someone who does good work for African Americans, or Hispanics, or women. Worse—and the reason the bill had a very real chance of failing—they will not compromise.

These days, it seems, you *have* to be extreme. It's all in on Trump or all against him. Radical left or dug-in right.

But there's another way.

THE ART OF THE COMPROMISE

Whether in politics or personal relationships, the word "compromise" can often be seen as a dirty word, a polite label for caving on a position that's truly important to you. But it doesn't have to be that way. Compromise isn't about finding a resolution that both parties can endure, even if they secretly hate it. It's about understanding where all parties in a disagreement are coming from and forging a solution that continues to meet the spirit of what each person truly wants—even if the details of that solution aren't what they first expected. While true compromise is rarely easy . . . sometimes it's necessary. When it is, these five tips I've learned might help.

1. Winning today is less important than winning your goal.

It's human nature to want to win, and the bigger the stage, the higher the stakes for that win. Whereas you might be willing to concede a point in a college classroom or at the kitchen table, giving up the floor at your workplace or in your church may feel impossible. And once you've won once, you want to keep winning, again and again. That implacable need to win, however, is already a failure. It shows you aren't truly committed to the longer-term goal of a successful relationship with those in your workplace, church, community, or family. Your driving need to dominate every minor decision could be setting you up for future discord that will keep you from accomplishing real, meaningful change. So be strategic as you enter each conversation, and know that sometimes compromising *is* the way to ultimate success.

2. Keep your emotions in check—except in this very important way.

We've all been in arguments with that individual who thinks the loudest voice or the greatest fury wins. Once again, this strategy can absolutely succeed in the short term—but in the long run, it wreaks havoc on your reputation as a negotiator or influencer. People want to work with others they can genuinely respect, even like. That's not the person whose rage is their most memorable attribute. Emotion does have its place in conversations while you're working toward compromise, but it's *not* after the fact, when everyone's laid out their viewpoint and you're struggling to reach an agreement. It's at the very beginning of the process. Specifically, when you first present your side of the story, explaining why you want the outcome you want. At that moment, you simply must . . .

3. Share deeply and authentically.

In any situation requiring compromise, all parties must get their say. The chance to explain their point of view and offer facts, research, or personal stories supporting their push for a particular outcome. It's critical to come prepared to state your case as clearly and authentically as you can, driving home the personal and deeply emotional reasons why you think the way you do. This is where skill as a speaker will come into play, and where you will most impress the other members of the group with how important and valid your position is. This is the area in which you have the most control.

4. Listen with an open mind.

Perhaps the simplest part of the process is to listen. Not with the intention of identifying logic lapses or argument holes, and not as simply a bridge before you get to speak again. Listen to opposing viewpoints with a genuinely open mind, giving yourself permission to learn something new about the topic that you perhaps had not considered before in that particular light. Listen actively, making eye contact with the speaker, taking notes if relevant, and even following up with questions that are not tailored to showcase your viewpoint, but to draw even deeper information from the speaker. This approach will get noticed and will earn you the respect of your peers even if they don't acknowledge it in the moment.

5. Show appreciation.

Ultimately, a decision will be reached and a resolution accepted. You may win this particular battle—or you may not. But no matter what the outcome is, be sure to show your appreciation to everyone involved in hammering out the compromise. All of you cared enough to make a good-faith effort to achieve the best solution, and the group's ability to work together ultimately will make it stronger, better prepared for the next decision you need to make. Take a moment to reflect on the final decision and why it's the best decision for the moment—and express those reasons positively and proactively. Compromise is hard work. Honor the effort, and you'll validate all parties involved.

6

ON MANY SIDES

HOLDING "OUR PARTY" AS ACCOUNTABLE AS THE OTHER

THEY CARRIED hundreds of torches, automatic rifles, standards emblazoned with swastikas and Iron Crosses. They waved Confederate battle flags in the street.

Nine months after Trump took office, the town of Charlottesville, Virginia, faced an unqualified tragedy. What began as a protest organized by self-described "white nationalists" grew into a massive gathering of neo-Nazis, neo-Confederates, southern nationalists, and alt-right militias from across the country. The morning after the now infamous parade of torches, protesters and counterprotesters met on the streets of downtown Charlottesville. By noon, Virginia governor Terry McAuliffe had declared a state of emergency.

Amid shouts of "Jews will not replace us" and "The South will rise again" and threats of "ovens" and "niggers' blood," guns were fired into crowds, cars became terrible weapons of hatred, forty people were sent to the hospital, and three people died. Yes, Childish Gambino, this *is* America.

Hours later, Trump spoke from the golf course near his vacation home in Bedminster, New Jersey. "There is no place for this kind of violence in America. Let's come together as one. We condemn in the strongest possible terms this egregious display of hatred, bigotry, and violence on many sides, on many sides."

On many sides. The phrase heard round the world.

Later, we'd learn that White House chief strategist Steve Bannon (co-founder of Breitbart News and alt-right patron saint) was the man behind the specific words chosen. Words clearly meant to call out some of the professional protesters and Antifa members from across the country who'd joined with genuine local counterprotesters.

At the time, I was working as a media surrogate for the White House. This meant I had a seat at the table. I participated in weekly conference calls and scheduled in-person meetings, where the White House would give us firsthand information about soon-to-break news and policies. As part of this arrangement, there was an expectation that I'd promote and defend the administration's agenda and talking points.

But in this case, I couldn't yet do that. The country had shattered, and Trump's first statement hadn't accomplished much of anything beyond implying that he blamed "many sides" equally.

I was in Chicago that day, and I put in a call to Kelly Sadler, a communications aide to President Trump. (Sadler would soon be fired for joking in a staff meeting that ailing Senator John McCain's opinion about the new CIA director "doesn't matter" because McCain was "dying anyway.")

"We need to have a conversation," I told her. "Trump's

statement isn't good enough. Far from it. He needs to get in front of the cameras and open up the national dialogue about race. Similar to what Obama did when he was running for president. I know Trump can't do it like Obama, but he needs to try. He needs to speak from the heart."

On the campaign trail, we'd all heard Trump talk about race in America in a way we hadn't seen in years—especially from a Republican. Trump didn't care about political correctness or saying the "wrong thing" one bit. It made him a loose cannon, sure, but it also meant he would discuss issues most politicians wouldn't in fear of a potential backlash.

Kelly agreed and assured me, "President Trump will get back in front of the cameras later today. Everything you're saying is absolutely correct, and he will rectify it at the next press conference."

"Okay, great," I said. "Keep me posted."

I got on a flight from Chicago to L.A. During the flight, I checked out my group chat of high-profile Republicans. Folk who worked in the Trump administration, in television, or in politics, fundraising, or lobbying. Most of the talk was about CNN and how its coverage of Trump in general was too biased and so on. I kept quiet.

While still on the plane, I got an email from *Fox & Friends*. They wanted me to go on the show the next morning to discuss the removal of Confederate statues. I was surprised they weren't inviting me on to discuss the riots or the neo-Nazis marching down American streets or Trump's statement. Still, I had a job to do. I agreed to go on and went about my day, business as usual.

Meanwhile, I wasn't the only Republican concerned about Trump's statement. Republican senators Ted Cruz, Jeff Flake,

Cory Gardner, Orrin Hatch, and Marco Rubio all called on Trump to *specifically* condemn the white supremacists and neo-Nazis. Senator Hatch tweeted, "My brother didn't give his life fighting Hitler for Nazi ideas to go unchallenged here at home," and Cruz wrote on Facebook, "The Nazis, the KKK, and white supremacists are repulsive and evil, and all of us have a moral obligation to speak out against the lies, bigotry, anti-Semitism, and hatred that they propagate."

Senator Gardner was among the first who argued that Trump needed to be clearer about whom he was condemning. "This is not a time for vagaries," he said. "This isn't a time for innuendo or to allow room to be read between the lines. This is a time to lay blame . . . on white supremacists, on white nationalism and on hatred."

I completely agreed with those senators. These were the more targeted words I'd been hoping for from Trump and why I'd called Kelly Sadler.

Shortly after I got back to L.A., I got word that Trump was giving another response. I knew this was a moment when we all needed to be brought together as a country, and it was my hope and expectation that he would set the right tone and alleviate the fears that many Americans of all stripes felt.

I caught the last half of his press conference, and I couldn't believe what I heard and saw. I listened to his words, studied his body language. I know race is a sensitive topic, hard to talk about. But it just seemed as if the president was defensive, or even excusatory . . . for the wrong people.

He said: "To anyone who acted criminally in this weekend's racist violence, you will be held fully accountable. Justice will be delivered. . . . Racism is evil. And those who cause violence in its name are criminals and thugs, including the KKK, neo-Nazis, white supremacists, and other hate groups that are repugnant to everything we hold dear as Americans."

I agreed with the words, but given the context, it felt like a standard "our condolences" statement, one that didn't speak to real concerns. And not at all what his aide had promised me hours earlier.

Let me find the first half of his speech, I thought, because I hadn't seen it from the very beginning. *Let me give him the benefit of the doubt.* I got online and watched the whole thing from the start.

Forty minutes later, I was even more upset than before.

"You had some very bad people in that group," Trump said, doubling down on his "on many sides" take. "But you also had people that were very fine people on both sides. You had people in that group that were there to protest the taking down of, to them, a very, very important statue and the renaming of a park from Robert E. Lee to another name."

Fine people on both sides? I was disgusted.

Here was the same man I'd gone on television to defend when I believed it was appropriate. While I hadn't been a supporter at the start of his campaign, he'd eventually convinced me he could be an effective president. Trump had proved to be a disrupter of the status quo during the primary and general election. Especially when he began to talk about issues of concern to black Americans. *Dems have taken your votes for granted! Black unemployment is the highest it's ever been! Neighborhoods in Chicago are unsafe!* All things I completely agreed with. But now he was saying, "I'm going to change all that!" He mentioned it at every rally, even though he was getting shut down by the leaders of the African American community. And what amazed me most was that he was saying these things to *white* people and definitely not winning any points there either. I'd defended Trump on more than one occasion and truly believed he could make a tangible difference in the black community. (And still do.) I'd lost relationships with family members, friends, and women I had romantic interest in, all because I thought advocating for some of his positions had a higher purpose.

But now the president of the United States had just given a group whose sole purpose and history have been based on hate and the elimination of blacks and Jews moral equivalence with the genuine counterprotesters. My grandfather was born and raised in Helena, Arkansas, where the KKK sought to kill him and other family members. You can imagine this issue was very personal to me. In Chicago, the day before Trump's press conference, my grandfather and I had had a long conversation about Charlottesville, and his words to me were fresh in my mind.

So, yeah, I was hurt. Angry. Frustrated. Sad.

And the hurt was personal for other reasons, too. Years before, I'd been in the Von Dutch store on the north side of Chicago one day. I was a young teenager and doing some shopping. Von Dutch was a big brand at the time, and I was fixed on buying a new baseball cap. The guy who ran the store had been checking me out the whole time. Eventually, he came up and got pretty aggressive. "Why are you here?" he asked. The question didn't make sense to me. He asked again, "What . . . are . . . you . . . *doing* here?"

I shrugged, still confused, and replied, "I'm just looking around."

"Get out of my store, nigger," he said.

That was the first time I'd heard racism expressed in such a hostile and direct way. That wasn't my only experience with racism and hostility. It hurt, and I can only imagine worse experiences that others have had. As Charlottesville played out, I well remembered how I'd felt that day in the store and other periods in my life.

But as I reflected on what the president could have done or said differently, I also remembered what it felt like in the weeks following 9/11. When, for a few glorious weeks, we were all united as Americans. For a brief time, it didn't seem to matter if you were black, white, or brown. We were all brothers and sisters because we were Americans. We shared certain values, a certain past, a certain goal.

We haven't really seen that since.

Charlottesville, I knew, had the same potential to unite us.

But Trump's response derailed that opportunity. America didn't need a stock statement. The country was pleading for a serious discussion about race, about our fundamental need to completely stamp out the Klan and neo-Nazis. I couldn't help but think of the 16th Street Baptist Church bombing and the Charleston church shooting. Emmett Till and Jimmie Lee Jackson. Black Codes and the Southern Manifesto.

Trump, I felt, had betrayed black America.

And Jewish America. And American decency.

So I got on social media and criticized him in a post. I wrote: "President Trump has just demonstrated on live national television that he does not understand race relations in America."

Innocuous enough, hardly calling him a "piece of garbage" or a "grand wizard," like others were doing. I put my comment on all my social media accounts.

The pushback was immediate. I got your standard snarky and mocking comments, some arguments. Some people stopped following me. Whatever.

I had to be on *Fox & Friends* the next morning at 3 A.M. Los Angeles time, so I left the online world and went to bed early. As I attempted to sleep, however, I couldn't stop thinking about what I'd just seen and heard.

I had no plans to discuss statues the following morning.

This wasn't about politics anymore.

This was our humanity.

I grew more and more emotional through the night. I couldn't sleep, so I paced my apartment while waiting to go on air. Hours later, not having slept, I got in the car and tried to hold it together on the way to the Fox News bureau. Waiting to start my segment, I wondered what the hosts of *Fox & Friends* would say about what had happened the day before, especially since this was reportedly one of Trump's favorite shows. How would they tackle it?

They hardly mentioned it. Merely said that Trump had spoken again. And I knew why. Because it was a train wreck.

I was up in the next segment, which was being moderated by Abby Huntsman (now a co-host of *The View*). Dr. Wendy Osefo, a liberal commentator and professor, spoke first. "I'm a mother of two black boys, and my heart bleeds," she said. Her words resonated with me, hitting me hard. I could do nothing but nod my head in agreement.

I tossed my planned talking points aside and decided to speak from the heart. I had to be extremely clear about my thoughts. I wanted to communicate directly to the president how this had impacted people across the country. The words just came out: "I come today with a very heavy heart. Last night, I couldn't sleep at all because President Trump, our president, has literally betrayed the conscience of our country . . . the very moral fabric in which we've made progress when it comes to race relations in America. . . . He's failed us."

I didn't know what I was going to say next. On the plane from Chicago to L.A., I'd prepared talking points about statues and citizens not taking the law into their own hands. But who would have thought he'd have a press conference like he had?

At that point in the show, I broke down in tears. The pain and sadness I felt, that our president, this man I'd defended on prior occasions, could not bring us together when the country so desperately needed it. I have, of course, never met anyone who lived through slavery, but I have met people who lived through Jim Crow. The anger and frustration I felt at this time made me feel as though we were back in those very dark times. After the segment was over, I wiped away my tears and got in the car. I needed sleep, needed to clear my mind and heart.

Heading back home, I got a call from Eboni K. Williams (my dear friend at Fox News). I couldn't believe she was calling me, because it was so early in the morning. Caught up in the swirl of emotions, I'd almost forgotten that half the country was already awake and that Eboni was calling from New York.

"I just watched," she said. "Are you okay?"

"No," I admitted, breaking down again.

She began to cry with me. "I'm so proud of you, Gianno," she said. "For speaking out and speaking your truth." She started going on about Trump, too. The words were heated; I'd never heard her curse before.

The next call was from Wendy, whom I'd just been on air with. She expressed her love and support as well. Here was a Democrat I'd been paired with to debate. Instead, the two of us were in full agreement.

I got home as the sun was rising and tried to finally get some sleep. No more than an hour passed before I popped back awake. Panic set in as I realized I'd likely set myself up to never be invited to do another TV appearance on Fox News again. They'd brought me on to talk about Confederate statues, and I'd turned into a blubbering guest saying how crappy Trump had been when his leadership was needed the most.

Fox News was only the number one news channel on earth, and I'd just bashed the president on his favorite morning program. Why would they ever have me back? I accepted that possibility. If there was a time I'd needed to represent the black community and my ideals for America, it had been then. If I'd lost the opportunity to appear again, it had been worth it, because I knew the president himself had likely been watching. Maybe, in some way, I had conveyed to him how millions of folk were feeling at that time.

Within the hour, I got a call from an unknown number. I picked up carefully. "Are you okay?" a man asked. In all honesty, I had no idea who it was, so I let him keep talking. "We were just talking about you in our staff meeting."

Awkward silence. I was still at a loss.

"It's Brian. Brian Jones." *What? Wait. Brian Jones? The president of Fox Business?* (And a fellow African American.) "I just wanted to check in on you," he said. "Charlottesville is so difficult for so many of us here. I'm so thankful you spoke out in such unequivocal terms."

He went on to tell me that he'd just been in their daily executive staff meeting and told everybody to watch that clip. What an amazing feeling to be supported like that.

I soon discovered that my on-camera commentary had gone viral, getting picked up by every major publication and network. I started receiving messages and calls from all over the country.

The New York Times. The Washington Post. For the first time in my career, I was on every national cable network that night—Fox News at seven, MSNBC at eight, CNN at ten—to talk about Trump's missed opportunity and the despair of Charlottesville, because so many people were moved by it.

Of course, not everyone was as supportive.

I lost many followers across social media. *Thousands.* They unfollowed me immediately, but not before sharing some thoughts. I got everything from "You're a disgusting ignorant nigger" to "I knew you were a Never Trumper."

I even got death threats. To me and my family.

Trump, I later learned, also was not pleased.

I got a call from the orbit of the White House. One of Trump's people said, "The president has seen the interview. What are you doing?"

I was soon after told that my services as a media surrogate for the White House were no longer needed.

I couldn't blame them. I'd been brought on to be a spokesman for them and had called Trump out on national TV in a way that everyone, at least for today, was talking about.

Conservative values will sometimes exceed a Republican president. Or governor or mayor. Conservative values will sometimes take precedence over the GOP.

Every day, I meet Republicans with widely differing views on everything from abortion to the death penalty, from immigration to the environment. There isn't some one-page flyer you get when you join the party that tells you exactly what you're supposed to believe on every issue. Yes, there are often consistent talking points, but part of being a good conservative is holding your own party accountable. If the values that first drew you to that party aren't being represented, it is imperative to speak up. It is only through such discourse and discomfort that true progress will be made. Even on Fox News, you'll sometimes hear people such as Sean Hannity or Ann Coulter ripping into the party for not following through on some promise or not standing up for an important issue.

Conservatism can be slow to change because its values are fundamental. But it does evolve to reflect changing times and needs critical voices to best adapt to that new reality.

Months after Charlottesville, it was reported that Trump said that press conference was the worst he'd ever given. I agree. I truly hope that he learned a serious lesson from the experience and that he, and others, will be better equipped to bring our country together in times like that in the future.

MY FIRST TIME questioning the party line was when I was working in the alderman's office at age fourteen. Back then, I aligned with the Democratic Party, because that's what you did in my community. One day at the office, I commented about how the politicians came around every year but nothing ever changed. The pushback was immediate. "That's because the white folk are the ones in power," I was told by the adults in the room. "That's why we can't get anything done. They don't want to give us anything. They give all the resources to the better communities downtown, and on the north side . . . where the white folk live."

To the people in that room, there was no other possibility. The Democrats who'd run inner-city Chicago for fifty years were apparently above blame, or even suspicion.

I asked, quite innocently, "Well, why don't we, you know,

take more control?" It was clear to me that most of the elected officials in my neighborhood were black. "What can we do without needing white help or approval?" They looked at me like I had two heads.

It doesn't matter whether you work in media, government, or a regular office. Few people question the status quo when they know what they say could put their jobs on the line. Too many leaders and politicians are in positions of power not because they're the best people for the job, but because they're the most likely to be controlled. Because they'll accept what the group is doing without question or objection.

An early mentor of mine in Chicago was a community organizer named Phillip Jackson, the founder of The Black Star Project (you met him in chapters 2 and 4). Phillip was a firebrand, passionate about the community and very ardent about ensuring the success of black people, especially young black men. One of his national initiatives was the Million Father March, where fathers, uncles, grandfathers, and father figures accompany children on their first day of school.

One year, he decided to run for state representative. The establishment hated to see him coming. They poured in a lot of resources, and he lost the race. But that didn't stop him from always being a thorn in the side of the Democrats. Jackson had made the national news because he drove around Chicago with an upside-down U.S. flag on his van to bring attention to all those black kids dying in the streets. "Where is President Obama?" he'd demand. He was really going hard on one of Chicago's own. "He's from here. What's going on? The kids in Chicago need Obama to step up!"

The Chicago Democrats were livid about his criticism. They begged him to stop and threatened his political ruin, but he wouldn't budge. Jackson even claimed that President Obama himself called and said he was "going to kick his ass" if Jackson didn't stop with all the TV appearances and attacks. He refused to toe the party line, and now the party was coming down on his head. Eventually, Jackson *did* stop driving the van around town, but he never stopped fighting for the community. To him, the needs of his neighbors always trumped political loyalties. And by following his convictions, he'd gotten Obama's attention. He'd moved the needle, moved the discussion forward.

During Obama's second term, I was working as an on-air analyst. I, too, had bought some into the hope and change rhetoric of his initial candidacy, but now the reality of his administration was clear for all to see. Here was a politician who'd failed to deliver on his promises. He'd clearly prioritized the Hispanic community, the gay community, and every other Democratic voting bloc he could think of *over* the African American community, who had supported him with 95 percent of their votes. More Americans, especially black people, were on food stamps than ever before. We had a loss of homeownership, and the unemployment rate for young black men climbed as high as 48.8 percent.

At that time, I was appearing on a cable TV program where two conservatives would square off against two liberals in a lively debate. Often, my conservative mate would call me out after the show. "It was three against one in there!" he'd complain, half joking but half not. "What are you doing?"

His assumption was that I would simply agree with him on every issue. To keep a united front, to keep things fair on air. As if there was only one way a conservative or a Republican would consider a topic.

After one show, my conservative partner stopped me in the greenroom. This time, he had a different, almost opposite, realization.

"I don't know how you do it," he said.

"Do what?" I asked.

"Go on every week and criticize Obama. To be honest," he said, "if I were black, there's no way I could do it. I would have an emotional attachment to this president."

On one hand, my debate partner expected me to toe the GOP line on every topic. And on the other, he expected me to support Obama because of the shade of my skin.

Yes, if he were black, he probably would have had a special attachment to the first African American president. I know I did initially. But that didn't mean I wasn't going to call Obama out when I thought he wasn't doing his job well. I wasn't going to confuse an "emotional attachment" with failed policy and moribund government. I was more than prepared for Obama to call and threaten to kick my butt as he had Phillip Jackson.

What I *wasn't* prepared for was my grandfather.

I assumed that he and the rest of my family were proud of me for making my way to D.C., starting my own firm, and now appearing on television as a political analyst. Despite all these leaps and bounds in my career, no one in my family had reacted to any of it. So one day, I straight up asked, "Granddad, aren't you proud of me?"

"Do you know what it's like," he asked, glaring, "when I hear what you say about Obama? I cringe."

It hurt my heart because this was my grandfather, somebody I looked up to more than just about anyone.

This was also the guy who often called out the Democrats on their nonsense—while still remaining a Democrat. He'd talk about how bad they were over at city hall or how politicians were always taking advantage of the community. He always told us about a time when Jesse Jackson invited the community to some big event on the South Side meant to expose how African Americans were being ripped off by their mortgage companies, being charged more because they were black. Jackson told folk to bring their mortgage statements to this meeting, so my grandfather went down with paperwork in hand. When he arrived, there was a brief prayer service and then a lot of talk, and he kept waiting to see when they were going to do the mortgage stuff. They never did. Instead, Jackson and his local crew were looking for donations.

My grandfather felt betrayed: "They were trying to rob our pockets and not trying to truly help." To him, it was another example of how the Jesse Jacksons and Al Sharptons of the world were out for themselves. They'd arrange picket lines to extort company X, and when the companies would buy them off, the issue would suddenly be resolved. Meanwhile, nothing truly changed for the neighborhood or those who'd walked the lines.

My grandfather often talked to *us* about that, but it didn't mean he'd ever talk about it in public or challenge his own party outside the confines of his own living room. Or be proud when I tried to do it for him.

THROUGHOUT MY CAREER, I've always tried to hold elected officials—in *any* party—accountable. When the Republicans took the House in 2016 but failed to deliver on a number of promises after a year, I went on TV and wrote columns to argue that the GOP had become derelict in its duty to the American people, unable to repeal and replace Obamacare, balance the budget, or get new tax and infrastructure bills passed.

My main target was the Freedom Caucus (a congressional caucus consisting of the most ultraconservative Republicans) for obstructing just about everything the GOP was trying to do. As one of its former members claimed, this supposedly ultra-conservative group would "vote no to the Ten Commandments" if given the chance.

The Freedom Caucus wasn't keeping its party in check for the good of the country. Rather, the caucus was determined to thwart any "Trump victory" at the *expense of* the country. I argued that Trump needed to break the back of the Freedom Caucus if he truly wanted to help the country and avoid becoming a one-term president.

I heard that one night when I was calling out the Freedom Caucus on Fox News, Geraldo Rivera was backstage listening to my segment with Meghan McCain. "Who is this kid?" Geraldo asked. "He's going places." It felt great to hear that. Geraldo is a legend and has managed to piss off (and challenge!) both parties equally for close to fifty years with his balanced investigative reporting and analysis.

I'm especially pleased when people email me or stop me on the street to say, "I watch you on TV and thank you for giving such a balanced view." At the 2019 White House Correspondents' Association Dinner in D.C., a Fox News fan stopped me outside the event to specifically thank me for being willing to call out when GOP policy or rhetoric doesn't match up with my conservative expectations.

In matters like fixing the healthcare system, reducing taxes and regulation, dealing with infrastructure issues, and ensuring social justice, there's only so long I can wait for something to get done. Only so many ways I can see my values ignored or twisted before speaking out.

Most television producers are looking for a particular take from their analysts and hosts, but only once, early in my career, has anyone ever tried to give me my talking points (an appearance that was ultimately canceled when I explained to the young producer that was not how things were done). For the most part, producers know their talent well and will only bring folk in on issues where they know where the analyst stands. That's being a good producer.

One producer told me that during an editorial planning meeting, a story came up and someone asked, "How about Gianno for that?" Everyone else in the room responded with a resounding "no." They knew me well enough to recognize the issues that get me fired up, the topics I'm most interested in— and where I stand on each of them.

AS A BLACK CONSERVATIVE in the public eye, I'm often forced to explain myself. Not only to the world but also to myself. I often deal with my own inner conflicts, struggling to determine where my loyalties lie. It's a constant dance, one of maintaining my integrity while preserving my identity. It's about being on a mission to serve my God, my country, and yes, my community— even though my black brothers and sisters sometimes don't see it as such.

I believe that the reason I've not been invited to certain mainstream Republican events as a speaker is that many party members want purebred Trump people right now. That's *all* they want. Gotta be a hundred percent pure. And if either George W. Bush or Calvin Coolidge were president, it'd be the same thing.

Since I was a teen, I've embraced the challenge of calling out my own team. As a Christian, as a black man, and as a Republican, I am as determined as ever to speak truth to power. It's more than okay to question your own party. It's, I'd argue, *required*. Everyone should seek opportunities to hold their own party to a higher standard.

Democrats screamed for Brett Kavanaugh to be denied a seat on the Supreme Court because of claims of a sexual assault, yet they looked the other way when sainted Bill Clinton was accused by multiple women of similar crimes.

For decades, African Americans have remained too loyal to Democrats and should hold them more accountable. White union workers and blue-collar types seem to have finally figured out that the Democrats aren't really delivering. The black community figured this out decades ago. But what will it take for African Americans to share their dissatisfaction publicly or express it in the voting booth?

My objective is not to be defiant just for the sake of being defiant. The "Never Trump" Republicans often fall into this category. Even when the president is achieving goals directly in line with conservative values—the First Step Act, two Supreme Court justices, the economy, low unemployment—this group still attacks him.

Fox News host Neil Cavuto, a mentor of mine, has gone viral the past few years thanks largely to his steady and laser-sharp Trump commentary, which holds the president fully accountable for his words and actions. In contrast, there are several Republicans who make a fine living by going on TV and bashing

Trump 100 percent of the time. They're of as little true value to progress as those Republicans who defend everything Trump does.

Whether we are Republicans or Democrats, the ultimate goal should be holding our leaders to the positions and objectives that best fit our aims for a better society. People are dug into their own corners. Right and left. Blue and red. We're more separated now than ever before, and the gap only continues to widen as technology allows us to create more and more ponds where only like-minded fish can swim: the cable news we watch, the websites we gravitate to, the people and groups we follow (and block!) on social media.

The idea of a Democrat and a Republican sitting across from each other for a balanced, or even civil, discussion almost sounds impossible anymore.

Perhaps the first step in that direction is to start holding *our own* party accountable. We may demonize the other side a little less once we start looking at our own team with a more honest eye and realize we're not perfect either. Before I could admit (shudder) that the other side had *any* good ideas that might advance my core values, I first had to accept the fact that my side sometimes has some bad ones.

That alone could be a big step toward both sides truly working together and unraveling some of the issues that both want resolved. Issues that are at the core of who we truly are beyond classifications and political tags.

First, however, we need the language to take that step.

7

NEWSPEAK

WHEN FREEDOM OF EXPRESSION GOES PC

"Don't you see that the whole aim of Newspeak is to
narrow the range of thought? In the end we shall
make thoughtcrime literally impossible, because there
will be no words in which to express it."

—George Orwell, *1984*

IN NOVEMBER 2018, I found out that someone wanted to kill me.

As a public figure, one involved in politics and national
TV, I've received my fair share of hate "mail." Nonspecific
death threats, name-calling, and once even a genuine and
highly detailed prayer for misfortune to befall me. But this was
different.

The FBI's Joint Terrorism Task Force, after examining the
forensic analysis, confirmed that I was one of the targets of pipe
bomb suspect Cesar Sayoc. Sayoc was the man arrested for
sending pipe bombs to Barack Obama, Hillary Clinton, Joe

Biden, actor Robert De Niro, billionaire George Soros, CNN, and other prominent Trump critics in the fall of 2018. Apparently, I'd been on the guy's hit list, too. The FBI told me Sayoc had "conducted specific open source research" on my name and address "indicative of targeting." His intent, they said, was to harm me. Whether it was my Charlottesville criticism or other things I'd said that were critical of President Trump that put me in his sights, I will likely never know.

What I do know is that the left and right tend to portray Sayoc differently. The left portrays him as a Trump supporter. In fact, he joined the Republican Party in his mid-fifties during the 2016 presidential primaries and drove a van covered in pro-Trump stickers. Numerous pundits on the right, however, have argued that Sayoc is some sort of "false-flag" operative for the left. I don't know. I know my inclusion on his target list muddies the waters of those easy narratives.

While I understand that we are all appropriately passionate about our political and cultural beliefs, I am disturbed by how that passion has morphed into vitriol and violence.

Antifa members routinely use physical violence against specific targets or those who disagree with their radical-left-leaning ideals. In Chicago in January 2017, four African American teens held a mentally disabled white teenager captive, torturing him for hours, and proudly posted videos of the act on Facebook with shouts of "F— Trump" and "F— white people." Shortly thereafter, a Chicago man named David Wilcox was brutally beaten by three men and then dragged behind a car as onlookers screamed, "Don't vote Trump!" Though Wilcox *did* vote for Trump, the attackers didn't know that when they beat him; they simply assumed he had because he was, as they put it, a "white boy." Most disheartening was that in both these instances, leaders on the left did not speak out against the attackers' actions. Their customary protesting was nowhere to be found.

If Hillary Clinton had won the general election and this had happened to some of her supporters, new laws would likely have been created to protect Clintonites. Yet the left wasn't saying, "Let's not attack Trump supporters." To the contrary, it seemed to be encouraging this kind of behavior time and time again. Multiple newspaper investigations have revealed that operatives working for the Democratic National Committee sent agitators to Trump campaign rallies in an attempt to cause violence—an effort that was supported by the Clinton campaign.

As anti-Trump hysteria consumed the left during the 2018 midterm elections, former attorney general Eric Holder advised: "When they go low, we kick them. That's what this new Democratic Party is about." Representative Maxine Waters (D-Calif.) directed: "If you see anybody from that [Trump] cabinet in a restaurant, in a department store, at a gasoline station, you get out and you create a crowd. You push back on them. Tell them they're not welcome anymore, anywhere!" Hillary Clinton agreed that you "cannot be civil" to members of the Republican Party.

Protesters routinely picket outside the homes of Fox News hosts. Prominent Republicans and their families are accosted while out in public or getting a bite to eat. Press secretary Sarah Sanders was infamously kicked out of the Red Hen, a Lexington, Virginia, restaurant whose co-owner couldn't bear to serve someone working in the Trump administration.

Of course, Republicans also behave badly toward Democrats. I certainly did not condone President Trump's heated rhetoric when as a candidate he joked, "If you see somebody getting ready to throw a tomato, knock the crap out of them, would you? Seriously, OK? Just knock the hell . . . I promise you I will pay for the legal fees."

But words and poster board can eventually morph into action and genuine violence.

A year into Trump's presidency, House majority whip Steve Scalise of Louisiana survived being shot in an attack as twenty-four Republican congressmen practiced for a charity softball event. The culprit was a known "left-wing activist" who belonged to numerous political Facebook groups, including Terminate the Republican Party, Donald Trump Is Not My President, and The Road to Hell Is Paved with Republicans.

All of this has led to everyday Americans fearing politically motivated violence. According to a 2017 study, approximately 76 percent of likely voters fear that politics will lead to violence. This includes 74 percent of Republicans and 83 percent of Democrats.

I believe there are two primary causes of this tendency toward violence.

The first is the heated rhetoric by leaders and mouthpieces on both sides. Their words and threats and demonizations can often drive those already too close to the edge—very often those suffering from emotional or mental issues—over the edge.

The second is the limitations brought on by the language of political correctness.

IN ITS BEST RENDERING, political correctness is a cultural effort to reduce or even eliminate language and behavior seen as marginalizing or insulting to disadvantaged or discriminated-against people. To think that only two decades ago, it was routinely acceptable to dismiss something lame as "gay" or to call a female co-worker "honey." To that extent, it's commendable that we're educating ourselves on "micro-aggressions" and becoming more aware of language, how it evolves, and how it can hurt others in unintended ways.

But far too often, today's PC is something else entirely.

According to Frank Ellis, a professor at the University of Sheffield, the term "politically correct" has roots in Leninist Russia and Nazi Germany, where to be politically correct meant using language in perfect accordance with the powers that be. Any language outside the approved scope of the leaders—or the mob—was thought to "impede the revolutionary spirit needed to upend the social order." In this sense, political correctness can devolve quickly into an attempt not to protect, but rather to stifle, conversation.

What's more, today technology allows citizens to live entirely within self-constructed echo chambers where the only voices they hear are those who think and believe exactly as they do. All other voices are blocked, unfriended, silenced, deemed too offensive to consider . . . or even to debate. Thus, we have colleges needing more and more "safe spaces" for those unwilling—or even unable—to listen to opposing viewpoints. Colleges where professors are afraid to share their life's work and worldview; where speakers (usually those on the right, such as right-leaning polemicists like Ben Shapiro and Ann Coulter) are often uninvited or chased away by angry mobs who believe that discussion and ideas should be determined by who shouts the loudest.

We've all heard the extreme, and absurd, examples of PC.

Inmates in Washington State prisons are called "students," and Seattle police are instructed to call suspects "community members."

Several school districts across the United States have banned *all* use of the words "boy" and "girl" as potentially offensive to students who may not identify as either.

Student leaders at the University of Oregon worked to remove Martin Luther King, Jr.'s famous "I Have a Dream" speech from a prominent school plaque because it didn't include a shout-out to those fighting for gender-identity equality. So preposterous that the words of King, a man who famously said, "Injustice anywhere is a threat to justice everywhere," would be taken down because he failed to advocate *specifically* for an injustice that wasn't even on our collective radar in 1963.

In one of the most amusing, or horrifying, examples of PC, the University of Wisconsin–Milwaukee declared that the terms "PC" and "politically correct" were themselves politically incorrect because they'd become pejoratives and so could be hurtful. I assume there were no actual adults in the room when that decision was made.

Extremes, for sure, but tinges of a truly Orwellian world in which people can draw from only a limited pool of sanctioned words when expressing their hopes, dissent, and ideas. If we don't support freedom of speech for those who offend us, then we truly don't support it at all.

A YEAR INTO the Trump presidency, a simple comment by the president led to a controversy that encapsulates the limitations of PC language.

Trump was at a rally in Huntsville, Alabama, for Republican senator Luther Strange. The president had won Alabama by a 2-to-1 margin and was deep within "Trump country." During his eighty-minute speech, he riffed on everything from the Crimson Tide to "Little Rocket Man," Kim Jong Un. Eventually, he waded into the debate about some NFL players who had been kneeling during the national anthem before games.

"Wouldn't you love to see one of these NFL owners," he asked as the crowd roared with approval, "when somebody disrespects our flag, to say, 'Get that son of a bitch off the field right now. Out! He's fired. He's fired!'" He went on: "You know, some owner is going to do that. He's going to say, 'That guy that disrespects our flag, he's fired.' And that owner, they don't know it [but] they'll be the most popular person in this country."

He went on to other matters, but the press zeroed in on the phrase "son of a bitch." Trump was calling the mothers of these NFL players female dogs, they proclaimed, further proof of his misogyny and—as the majority of NFL players are African American—his profound racism. Politicians and pundits and NFL players (former and current) quickly took to the airwaves and web.

"Of course, 'son of a bitch' is an insult that's usually not taken literally," one pundit wrote. "But, Donald Trump is President of the United States of America. . . . Everything he says must be taken literally. And last night he literally insulted the mothers of NFL players protesting racial injustice, calling them female dogs."

Come on. If you want to mock or question the president for using such coarse language, that's one thing. But implying that the use of this phrase—in the context of a raucous rally among supporters—should be taken literally, when clearly that was not Trump's intent, is absurd.

It gets in the way of real change. It ends real discussion.

The issue rival politicians and pundits *should* have focused on that night wasn't the president's use of this common, though perhaps offensive, phrase but the larger issues of freedom of expression, institutional racism, and building trust in inner cities between police and the citizens they are supposed to protect.

But those are tough issues to talk about or solve. Unfortunately, it's far easier to focus on the low-hanging fruit of some poorly chosen words plucked from a lengthy speech. That's the real danger of PC culture. The hours spent discussing Trump's use of "son of a bitch" could have been better spent debating and untangling the harder issues at hand.

This is part of the criticism I, ironically, leveled at NFL quarterback Colin Kaepernick and the other kneeling athletes. On TV and in print, I supported their right to protest, but I was openly against their use of the flag to do so. I also questioned what would come next. On air one night, I suggested that Kaepernick and other NFL stars who supported this form of protest should head to Capitol Hill to seek reforms and effect *real* change through use-of-force laws. That night, ESPN host Stephen A. Smith praised my take on Twitter, and we had dinner in New York City the following week to discuss it.

Those truly serious about resolving an issue should take it beyond the initial protest, beyond the criticism of a specific phrase, and do something. Foundations are great, and many NFL players *have* donated their time and millions of dollars to their communities. Beyond the money, though, it's important for them to use their celebrity to get in people's faces on Capitol Hill or in state capitols across the country to try to change the laws and thus create *real* change.

All too often, discussions of race and discrimination are pursued not for genuine reasons, but for counterfeit, low-cost, convenient political posturing.

Sometimes, they're even manufactured.

You may remember a story that played out in Chicago in early 2019. An up-and-coming young black actor named Jussie Smollett was allegedly attacked near his apartment in the Streeterville neighborhood. Two men in ski masks, he claimed, tossed bleach on him, put a noose around his neck, called him racial and homophobic names, beat and bit him, and then shouted, "This is MAGA country!" It turns out, however, that Smollett staged the whole thing and his two attackers were his physical trainers, two brothers from Nigeria. Before the "attack," the brothers were taped in a Chicago department store asking if the store had any MAGA caps. What a farce. What a sideshow. What a heartbreak.

For me, as a black man from Chicago, this story was far more serious than an actor looking to get his name better known. What Smollett did was methodical and strategic, drawing on the darkest side of PC politics. He wanted half of America to believe that guys in MAGA hats had done this to him. He wanted the networks to cover his lie for days so that people would fear the world around them even more. I truly believe that this was a hate crime against the conscience of our country and that it could have caused violence. Smollett well knew that many Americans feel that we're living on a racial and political powder keg. Days after the staged assault, he "bravely" took the stage and told a sold-out crowd of fans at the Troubadour rock club in West Hollywood, California, that he was "gonna stand strong with y'all" and that he "couldn't let those motherfuckers win."

Those "motherfuckers," in Smollett's worldview, are anyone who voted for Trump. That's more than 62 million Americans. It was a dishonest, unhelpful narrative. And the way he played that narrative out was completely dependent on the one-sided way in which PC politics usually functions.

Meanwhile, the number of hate groups in the United States today was already at a twenty-year high. Antiblack hate crimes increased by 16 percent between 2016 and 2017 and accounted for 28 percent of all hate crimes. Smollett's actions made every black person in this country unsafe. His scam, once it was exposed, allowed for more people to approach *genuine* hate crimes with more skepticism. He cried wolf, and the rest of us could pay the price.

Right around the time Smollett was doubling down on his best acting role yet, Virginia governor Ralph Northam was dealing with a nightmare of his own. A photo from his 1984 medical school yearbook page showed two students posed together, one grinning in blackface and the other in a KKK hooded cape. Northam was clearly one of the students, although for a few days he denied it. Then he admitted that he "may" have worn blackface "once" in a dance competition as Michael Jackson. Eventually, he acknowledged that it probably *was* him in the picture, but that he had no memory of it.

At the end of the day, none of this mattered.

Because Governor Northam is a Democrat.

There would be no *serious* calls for his resignation, no stripping of his duties, no moral outrage from the party built on "protecting minorities." In fact, the opposite seemed to happen. Democrats rushed to his *defense.*

Support came from a range of Democrats, from former vice president Al Gore to Gregory McLemore—a city council member in Franklin, Virginia, and one of the state's senior African American leaders—who said: "We need to support our fellow Democrats. United you stand, divided you fall. I can't [forsake]

Gov. Northam for acting white in America." It was a surprisingly candid defense based on the apparent assumption that *all* white people are inherently racist, so let's give "our" white guy a break.

This support from fellow Democrats clearly helped Northam. Following the revelation, a *Washington Post* poll showed that almost 60 percent of African Americans in the state of Virginia wanted him to remain in office. If Northam stepped down, Democratic lieutenant governor Justin Fairfax would have replaced him. But Fairfax was in the middle of his own sexual harassment scandal. Then what about the next person in line, Democratic attorney general Mark Herring? Nope, he *also* wore blackface as a young man. Three Democrats accused of crimes similar to those liberals have accused Trump and others on the opposite side of the aisle of committing. Next up would have been the Speaker of the Virginia House of Delegates, Kirk Cox, a Republican. No chance.

And so Northam began his apology tour. The liberal brain trust—both white and black—took it as an "opportunity to advance the cause of African Americans rather than wallow in the punitive measures of revenge, which we know wouldn't fly if Northam was a Republican." Northam remains in office at the time of this writing.

Did the Democratic leadership really have no choice but to look the other way on this? I'm not arguing that anyone who ever wore blackface should be banned from a prominent job. (I think the memo that blackface is, and always was, racist has now been distributed.) The problem is the way the issue has been used as nothing more than a political football.

When Democrat and former Senate majority leader Harry Reid praised presidential candidate Obama's "light-skinned" appearance and speaking patterns "with no Negro dialect, unless he wanted to have one," liberals kept mum. And when Northam, a liberal, finally admitted that he'd worn blackface, or had possibly been the one in the KKK uniform, it was called a "learning opportunity." But when conservative talk show host Megyn Kelly attempted to *discuss* blackface, saying that kids back in the 1970s didn't know any better, she got fired.

Imagine if it had been a Republican governor in blackface. Are you kidding? The Democrats and the national media would have gone absolutely crazy. Jail time would likely have been recommended, and the GOP would have been forced to respond quickly—and decisively.

This isn't even hypothetical. When Republican representative Steven Arnold King of Iowa asked *The New York Times,* "White nationalist, white supremacist . . . how did that language become offensive?" and then commented that the new Democrat-controlled House was "no country for white men," the Republican Steering Committee immediately removed him from all House committee assignments. Conservative commentators like Ben Shapiro called for King to be censured and for the representative to be challenged in his next primary. The GOP certainly knows it has a PR problem in this regard, so they moved quickly to send a message.

But the Democrats, who feel they already have minority votes guaranteed . . . not so much. Why was Bernie Sanders one of the only white liberals to call out Hillary Clinton for referring to inner-city teens (*black* teens) as "super predators" back in 1996? During Clinton's 2016 run for president, Black Lives Matter activists demanded an apology for this comment from the front-running candidate.

We must no longer see racism and PC as political bullets, to be used only on our enemies. If we really want to effect change, we need to hold both sides accountable. When we weaponize racism (or sexism, or any other ism), the underlying message always gets lost. So does the chance for any real change.

That was the true tragedy of what Jussie Smollett did. There are enough *real* injustices against minorities without having to invent them. Gandhi and MLK didn't have to *invent* injustices and violence to prove there was something in our world that needed to be fixed. All they had to say was: *Look, I'm going to show you what's really going on, and I trust you to figure it out.*

Even after Smollett's lie was revealed, liberal activists were still pushing his narrative. *But . . . what about the Chicago police?* they said. *But . . . what about the murder of Laquan McDonald?*

When the left gets more honest about whom they point fingers at and what moral outrage they'll pursue in a given week, America will be better able to focus on the real issues facing our country, the real moral outrages we should all be working on together.

FOR TOO LONG, Republicans (*and* conservatives) have been fearful of going into certain communities—specifically the African American community. They worry that they will say the "wrong thing" and get labeled as racists. At a time when conservative ideals are precisely what the African American community needs to hear, when the Democrats and big government have taken blacks for granted for generations, the GOP largely remains afraid to talk.

One reason for this, I think, is that the language has been taken from them.

And so nothing changes. And more people suffer.

Trump, for all his hard edges and blustering and coarseness, has never cared about political correctness—whether we like it or not at times. Before that speech in Alabama, he had called plenty of people SOBs, from *Meet the Press* moderator Chuck Todd to Senate minority leader Chuck Schumer. Both of whom are white.

From day one, part of Trump's appeal was that he was the "anti-PC candidate." A throwback to a time before people were afraid to talk.

Does this bring with it some cringeworthy moments? Oh, yes. Especially for Trump.

But it also usually brings needed conversation.

Candidate Trump was a very "politically incorrect" individual. When it came to the Republican playbook, he threw it out the window. Especially when campaigning and reaching out to communities that normally do not support the GOP. Trump often spoke of things that were fairly polarizing and previously "forbidden" for Republicans to address. That Chicago is a violent city: the failing schools, the drugs, the unusually high unemployment rate for African Americans. That cities run by Democrats have, for more than fifty years, proved to be historically and statistically bad for black people. Topics that most other Republicans refused to talk about because they were on the edge of being "politically incorrect" or "racist."

Chicago is violent, you say? (How racist!)

Gangs have filled the void left by businesses and taken over much of the city? (How racist!)

A whopping 77 percent of African American children are born out of wedlock, and that is an issue? (How racist! *And* misogynistic!)

Whether it's Trump saying such things or CNN's Don Lemon (an African American who waded into the out-of-wedlock issue at one point), the reaction is the same. *How dare you? This is outrageous. Your language is offensive.*

But, in truth, the *words* aren't the problem. Rather, a culture that perpetuates, excuses, and ignores major issues is the problem. The facts on the ground are *more* offensive.

Attacking one sentence or word is easy. Confronting the reality connected to that sentence or word is hard. It requires real discussion and debate. Real thought.

And then real effort.

For too long, leaders have avoided addressing difficult issues for fear of being labeled racist or xenophobic. This causes GOP candidates to ask, all too often: *Why should I work for votes in the black community when I know the likelihood is that the people there are never going to vote for me and probably will label me a racist?* It's a lose-lose situation.

You've failed, candidate Trump basically told the Democrats and local leaders. *You've failed this community.* He spoke about inner-city problems even at events in farming areas of the Midwest that are mostly white, and he used the media to get his message out. Without regard for what the left might call him or how nervous his white audiences might get.

The result was that Trump garnered more black and Hispanic votes than Romney or McCain had in the previous two presidential elections and also reached double-digit support (13 percent) among black men. My analysis: African Americans *do* want alternatives to the Democratic Party, but legitimate efforts must be made.

This was exactly the kind of outreach I'd been advocating for years. In my role as African American outreach director for the DuPage County Republican Party, my entire purpose had been to speak to the black community as a conservative, knowing that many of them already held most of the same values I did. In comparison with Trump, it was harder for them to call me a racist. I spoke to groups like the NAACP and other historically black (and Democratic) organizations. I did so because I wanted my community to know there were solutions and synergy to be found in the Republican Party.

ACCORDING TO a study published in 2018 in *The Atlantic*, some 80 percent of Americans have a negative view of PC culture and the dangerous paths and objectives it pursues. No wonder Trump's anti-PC stance has found an audience. The numbers are similar even among younger Americans: 74 percent for ages twenty-four to twenty-nine, and 79 percent for those under twenty-four.

There is a reason for this. Eighty percent of Americans understand that the cornerstone of a free society is the free exchange of ideas.

"If liberty means anything at all," George Orwell wrote in response to communist Russia, "it means the right to tell people what they do not want to hear." Lenin, a radical communist, called free speech "a bourgeois prejudice."

President Kennedy declared, "We are not afraid to entrust the American people with unpleasant facts, foreign ideas, alien philosophies, and competitive values. For a nation that is afraid to let its people judge the truth and falsehood in an open market is a nation that is afraid of its people."

A hundred years earlier, Frederick Douglass argued, "Liberty is meaningless where the right to utter one's thoughts and opinions has ceased to exist. That, of all rights, is the dread of tyrants. It is the right which they first of all strike down."

Western culture and democracy have depended on the open exchange of ideas for thousands of years. The Enlightenment writer Voltaire, a guidepost to Thomas Jefferson and other founding fathers, was famously summarized as believing: "I disapprove of what you say, but I will defend to the death your right to say it." And, as far back as ancient Greece, which practiced democracy in its earliest form, the poet Homer wrote: "To speak his thoughts is every freeman's right, in peace and war, in council and in fight."

America is a nation of free citizens who must have the right to be heard . . . *and* to hear. Free speech, as guaranteed in our Bill of Rights and in the United Nation's Universal Declaration of Human Rights, is intended to protect the controversial and even hurtful word, and not just, as General Colin Powell put it, "comforting platitudes too mundane to need protection."

Conservatives know that freedom of expression has survived the test of time. It does not cower before the shouts of a mob or the threats of a single oligarch. It does not tremble before today's cultural demands, because it is adaptive. Just as with a free market of goods and services, conservatives trust that a free market of information and ideas and words will produce, in the end, the best product for each individual and for society as a whole.

If a person is truly racist, I want them to be direct and tell me what's on their mind. Political correctness prevents that.

I never expected my own political views or words would put me in the sights of someone whose intent was to harm me and others he disagreed with. Other eras brought us bombings, students murdered at Kent State, and assassinations of politicians and civil rights leaders. Which is why we all should exercise extreme caution and consider the words we use, endeavoring not to inflame the passions of those who misunderstand. And at this point every side—especially those in prominent positions—should adhere to responsible speech, because words matter and sometimes the ramifications can be deadly.

In truth, it's a small minority attempting to curtail our language and create the dictionary we must all use. Fervid voices within the media and academia. Most often radical-left-leaning individuals who truly believe their worldview is so correct that no other views should be heard.

Even President Obama spoke against this.

At an Iowa town hall in 2015, Obama famously spoke of the "coddling" going on in too many of America's colleges and universities. "Sometimes," he said, "there are folks on college campuses who are liberal, and maybe even agree with me on a bunch of issues, who sometimes aren't listening to the other side, and that's a problem, too. I've heard of some college campuses where they don't want to have a guest speaker who is too conservative or they don't want to read a book if it has language that is offensive to African Americans or somehow sends a demeaning signal towards women. I gotta tell you, I don't agree with that either. I don't agree that you, when you become students at colleges, have to be coddled and protected from different points of view. I think you should be able to see—anybody who comes to speak to you and you disagree with, you should have an argument with 'em. But you shouldn't silence them by saying, 'You can't come because I'm too sensitive to hear what you have to say.' That's not the way we learn either."

Even after Trump's election, Obama held true to this position. When asked about Trump's stance that political correctness has gone too far, Obama told NPR, "If somebody says, 'You know what, I'm not sure affirmative action is the right way to solve racial problems in this country,' and they're immediately accused of being racist, well, then I think [Trump has] a point." He agreed that some on the left (*and* on the right) often use political correctness to shut down debate over legitimate issues—a problem, he says, that "has hurt political discourse." I don't agree with President Obama on much, but I certainly agree with him here.

Too many people—white, black, and brown—have told me that they're afraid to speak up because they're afraid of being called racist or accused of "playing the race card." People don't want to feel that kind of pain. To end up as an Internet meme. They don't want to lose everything.

So we stay silent and remain suspicious of one another.

Think about the whites who dared question Jussie Smollett's obvious lies. People cried, "You're just a racist." Such remarks keep us divided.

Only when people feel comfortable discussing race or gender or creed or socioeconomic status honestly will true change occur. When Americans can freely talk to one another, and listen, and allow for those uncomfortable moments that happen in a free society. Such communication does not come from the position that what came before me *must* be wrong; that what my opponent is proposing *must* be wrong; that only my team's words are correct and all others are racist, sexist, microaggressive, threatening . . .

To those people who believe such things, I invite you to the public forum. There, you and I—and anyone else who wishes to—will speak of such matters. Maybe, just maybe, we'll come to understand one another a little better.

8

THE SEEDS OF CHANGE

THE OVERLOOKED POWER OF AN ACTIVE FAITH

"Faith without works is dead."

—James 2:26

NANA, THE GRANDMOTHER (on my mother's side) who raised me, was a highly religious woman. A self-proclaimed pastor, a dedicated evangelist, and a woman who spoke in tongues, she had tried almost every Christian denomination there was, usually taking me and my eight siblings along. We often spent an entire Sunday cooped up inside some neighborhood church. I recall one service that started at 7 A.M. and kept going . . . and going . . . and going . . . until finally we made our way home on the public bus around 10 P.M.

For years, Nana led services in her own home for a congregation of maybe ten people. But her real dream was to find a spiritual home that would give her the recognition she thought she deserved as a community pastor.

When you're a pastor in the black community, you're a celebrity of sorts. There aren't a whole lot of business owners, entrepreneurs, professors, or politicians walking around in neighborhoods like the one where I grew up. Religious leaders are often the most successful and important people African Americans have an opportunity to interact with. And when the pastor visits you at home, that is a very big deal. Nana wanted to have that same level of importance in her community. When the churches we visited didn't give her the recognition she desired, we'd move on to another congregation. (This dangerous cycle reverberated throughout our lives and into other areas. When our feelings got hurt or we faced criticism, we'd run away instead of facing the issue head-on.) We must have visited forty churches in this way.

Meanwhile, I began to dislike going to church. Like lots of people—especially those raised in African American churches, where the services go on for hours—I felt as if I was spending too much time in church without getting anything out of it. Like many families, we prayed before every meal ("God is good, God is great . . .") and before going to bed. Nana also used to have us read from the Bible every morning before we went out—Psalm 23, Psalm 51, Psalm 91—as protection against whatever awaited us outside the front door. But instead of treating these activities as something precious, a genuine faith-based opportunity to get to know God, I felt like we just did them for the sake of tradition. As kids, we were told *what* to do instead of learning *why* we did it.

Nana's faith promised that "one day" things would be better, that we wouldn't be poor anymore. "God will save us," she always said. In the afterlife, sure. But we also needed saving right then.

Despite spending more time in church than the Plymouth Pilgrims, there were times we couldn't make the rent, times the lights, gas, and water were shut off. I didn't believe children of the living God should be in that position. Year after year, I looked for some financial salvation. I'm not talking about some "let me get rich because I believe in God" thing. But I expected more from my marathon sessions of piety. The struggle was so real, I can understand how people lose faith.

Clearly, I'm not the only one who has ever felt this way. While almost 80 percent of Americans claim to have a religious affiliation, fewer than half report that they attend church. The real number (taken from churches, not the polling of supposed churchgoers) may be as low as 20 percent.

So 80 percent of Americans believe in God, but only 20 percent go to church to spend time with Him and their fellow believers. There's a major, and heartbreaking, disconnect here.

And a truly missed golden opportunity.

Because, when the rubber really meets the road, the reason I've had success in my life isn't because I look pretty good in a suit or even because I'm willing to grind to get the next break (though both of those things are true). Instead, as I look at my life and the lives of the people around me, I've come to believe that one of the most overlooked resources for combating poverty and disillusionment resides not in the halls of government or the boardrooms of corporations, but inside the four walls of the church.

WHEN I WAS SEVENTEEN, I became close with my Aunt Patricia. Everyone on my dad's side of the family looked up to her. She'd moved out of Chicago in 1986, the year I was born, going two thousand miles away to Los Angeles at a time when few people in my neighborhood ever moved more than a couple miles from the block. Aunt Patricia had been in the military, seen the world, gotten a six-figure job in technology. I don't know what you're used to seeing, but on the South Side of Chicago in the 1990s, she was as close to a hotshot as we were ever going to see.

Whenever we talked, I would ask Aunt Patricia for advice on dating, on school, on life in general. She always gave me advice without ever being judgmental. Eventually, we got to the subject of faith.

My aunt is not a religious person in the traditional sense. I'd never once talked to her about Christianity—she kept quiet about such things—but I knew her faith was different from the loud, in-your-face *Praise Jesus!* marathons I'd gotten used to on Sundays. It was more about her actions than the show.

One day, I asked Aunt Patricia a question about developing my own faith more, and she replied simply: "What did God tell you?"

I had no idea what she was talking about. Growing up, I had heard people claim that God had told them this or that, but it was mostly the pastors and faith leaders who claimed such things.

"What did God tell me?" I said, laughing. "That's why I'm calling you! To find out what He said."

"No," she said. "*You* have to have a relationship with Him for yourself."

"Okay," I went along. "So how do I hear from God?"

My aunt said I should pray. Then she gave me some scriptures to read. In fact, for the next several months, no matter what issue I came to her with, she had a suggestion for my next reading.

Tough decision to make? Proverbs 3:5–6

Looking for a job? Psalm 75:6

Jealous? Proverbs 14:30

Had an accident? Psalm 34:20

I started to read the same scriptures over and over, pen in hand, writing down my reactions and any questions that came to mind. Afterward, I'd go to her with a consideration or issue, and she'd say again: "What did He say?" Often, I would tell her what I *thought* God had said, and she'd counter, "No, that's not what God said."

I was irritated. How did she have any idea what He had or hadn't said?

"Well, that's against this scripture and this scripture and this scripture," she would say. "And God is not the 'author of confusion.' " It was a quote from 1 Corinthians. "He would not tell you something that goes against His words."

I was astounded. She saw the Bible as the direct conduit to a personal relationship with God. There was no middleman. No pastor or church. No congregation or dogma. Just me and my Bible and whatever voice or direction I might one day hear if I kept at it.

Shortly after I began studying and praying through the Bible, I had a car accident. My insurance company didn't cover it, so I was left with damages to pay and no car to drive. Something so simple became a chance to put my newfound faith into action. I needed to manifest God's help in this matter, because the insurance company sure wasn't going to help.

I'd just turned eighteen. It was summer. Every morning, I'd wake up at 5 A.M. to pray and read the Bible, then take several buses to work at the Social Security Administration center in downtown Chicago. At lunch, I'd pull out my Bible again. Same thing after dinner. This went on all summer. After reading the scriptures, I'd pray: "Father God, I thank you and praise you for you told me that if I delight myself in you, you would give me the desires of my heart [Psalm 37:4]. I thank you and praise you that my path has been directed, and I receive this new car in Jesus's name."

Sure enough, the car funds were starting to build, and I was beginning to truly believe. By the end of the summer, I'd earned enough money to pay off the damaged car and purchase a new one. It's not like a satchel of unmarked bills showed up on my nightstand after I prayed. But God had provided ideas and opportunities for extra work and income that I'd embraced with open arms. These were the practical real-world results I'd been looking for as a child.

But that was only a start. What happened next changed my life.

One Saturday morning, I was on my way to visit a friend (a pastor's daughter, fatefully) when I heard—and I believe to this day, this was the Holy Spirit—a voice: *Go visit Aaliyah.*

Aaliyah was my best friend from the seventh grade. I hadn't seen her in weeks, but the command to visit her *right now* had come as clearly as if the speaker were standing right next to me. So I turned and started walking. After all, Martin Luther King, Jr., said: "Faith is taking the first step even when you don't see the whole staircase."

But when I got to my friend's house, her mom was the one

who answered the door. "Sorry, Aaliyah's not here," she said, smiling.

I was confused. *Had I imagined the whole thing?* I expected some kind of grand revelation or a once-in-a-lifetime message from my friend. But all I got was me standing on the porch with her mom in the doorway, looking at me with equal confusion. I wasn't yet seeing the second step of this staircase.

"Okay," I said, retreating. "It was good seeing you." I continued on to my original destination and spent much of the day trying to guess what, if anything, I had manifested by being obedient. That voice! Had I avoided a shooting? Getting hit by a car? I didn't know.

Around 10 P.M., I was riding the bus home when, all of a sudden, I felt thirsty. I knew there was a Walgreens at 111th and Michigan, but as the stop came into view and I stood to get off the bus, I heard the same voice again: *Don't get off the bus.* The voice was as clear as the one I'd heard earlier in the day. This time, however, I didn't listen. When the bus stopped, I got off.

What happened next is where I might lose some of you, but that's okay.

It's common for us to disregard anything outside the normal narrative. Church, for many, is merely "going to church" because it's "a good thing to do." For some, it might offer a temporary motivational change. A passing feel-good experience as opposed to a life-changing one. I understand. I once thought the same.

This day, however, I learned another way.

I'd made it maybe fifteen feet down the street before I came across a man propping himself up with a two-by-four in the middle of the sidewalk. He was shirtless and looked like one of the neighborhood gang members. I'd grown up on the South Side and had seen much, much worse in my days, so I didn't think much of it and prepared to walk around him.

"You got a dollar?" he asked, his voice garbled as if his mouth was full of dirt.

"Sorry, I don't have one to give you," I said.

I passed him, but by the time I made it another few steps, the guy started yelling: "He has a dollar! He has a dollar!"

Now I understood: *I'm in it.* I started jogging because the Walgreens was right there. Then I heard someone running behind me—a *couple* of someones—and my jog became a full-on sprint.

I made it through the parking lot, to the front door of Walgreens. But when I kicked my feet toward the sensors, the door didn't open. Walgreens was closed. *God help me,* I thought, and turned around.

Two grown men—the shirtless guy and a pal—were now both directly in front of me. "You think I'm a bitch, huh?" the first guy taunted. Both men put their hands up and motioned to hit me.

Without even thinking, words just came out of my mouth: "No weapon formed against me shall prosper, and every tongue that raises against me, God shall condemn it!"

The men staggered backward away from me. Something had pushed them—something invisible. I'm not joking. It might sound hard to believe, but the only explanation I have is that some kind of angel had intervened on my behalf. Had to. Suddenly, the men were far enough back for me to get past them.

I was shocked. My mind swirled in a hundred directions. *What had happened?* The words I spoke were scriptures I had studied that summer. Isaiah 54:17. With no explanation, I suddenly spoke again: "Out of the abundance of the heart, the mouth speaks." Another scripture!

My two attackers stood, bewildered and angry.

Run! I heard that still small voice cry.

So I ran.

Another group of men had emerged, about ten strong. The shirtless man looking for a dollar now had half the block chasing after me.

Before I got very far, I saw a black Monte Carlo stopped a short way ahead, a car packed with guys inside. I started running toward them for help. *Don't,* I heard. *Keep running.* But the car was right there. It made no sense to keep running. I might get some help from these guys right here and now. I slapped my hands on the car window and breathlessly asked for help. The guys inside just stared at me briefly, then looked away to their own matters. Meanwhile, my pursuers had gotten closer. I ran again, for blocks. I'd gained some ground on them again.

Where do I go? I wondered.

Laundromat, I heard.

I know what you're probably thinking. Crazy, right? But that's the point. Because a block later, I came upon an open laundromat. I figured I could hide in there for a bit, let these guys pass, and maybe sneak out afterward. *Go!* the voice said. There were many doors to the laundromat, but I felt led to go through the one that was the farthest away from me.

As I burst through the laundromat door, looking for a place to hide, looking for someone who might help, the first person I saw inside was . . . my best friend's mother.

That's right. The same woman I'd met earlier in the day on that random visit to Aaliyah's. "Gianno!" She stared, eyes wide. "What in heavens are *you* doing here?" It was close to 11 P.M.

The story spilled out of me, and she went into immediate action. She gave me her car keys and told me to drive straight to her house. When I got there, her boyfriend told me to wait while he went back to the laundromat and checked things out. When the two of them returned together, they told me that "ten guys came into the laundromat with bats and two-by-fours," looking in the bathroom and under the tables. They were looking for me and likely wanted to kill me. (This happened near the same block where a teenager named Derrion Albert was beaten to death with a piece of railroad tie some years later.) I was shaking.

I couldn't believe everything I'd just experienced. The voice. The invisible shove. The directions to my friend's mom, who saved me that night. When I finally made it home, I called my aunt in Los Angeles. "Oh my God," I said. "This thing is real."

Folk like Mike Pence and George W. Bush are often mocked, especially by liberals, for claiming "God speaks to" them. Interesting how the mocking is silenced when Oprah Winfrey claims the same. Within a couple months, God had helped me out with the car *and* likely saved me from being beaten to death. I wanted to know even more about this God. I wondered: *What else can He and I do?*

Fortunately, when the student is ready to learn, the teacher will appear.

ONE DAY, MY AUNT SUGGESTED: "You should go listen to Bill Winston."

Who? I'd never heard of him, so I looked him up. Winston was a conservative pastor of a twenty-thousand-member church in Chicago. No, more like in the *suburbs* of Chicago. By now you know what I think about the suburbs—plus I had a half dozen excuses for not going. The drive was too far, and I didn't want to attend a big church. Despite everything I'd just experienced, a genuine miracle that likely saved my life, my aunt's advice fell on deaf ears.

Thankfully, I used to fall asleep with the TV on, usually watching music videos on BET. A month or so after being chased, I woke to a deep, serious, powerful voice on TV discussing the blessing of Abraham. The voice talked about Abraham's journey and how all Christians are descended from him. I sat up in bed, listening intently. This guy, whoever he was, was pretty dynamic. I'd never heard or seen anyone like him. There was a phone number at the bottom of the screen to call to get a CD of the sermon. *Do I really want to pay for a church tape?* I thought. But I called anyway.

The mystery pastor was, of course, Dr. Bill Winston.

His sermons on Abraham came in a series of three CDs and cost $30. Remember, I was eighteen years old and had spent the summer climbing out of debt. *Thirty dollars for a church tape?* I thought. *No. No. Try again.* But I ordered the CDs reluctantly, and when they showed up a few days later, I started listening. It was so good. Pastor Winston built his sermons on a foundation of scripture. Like any good teacher, he stayed focused, exploring different iterations of the same text. I really learned. He explored the Greek, Aramaic, and Hebrew roots of words in the different versions for a better understanding.

And he stressed the act of *doing,* of bringing God into your everyday life. Winston taught that faith is *now.* For example, if you say "I am going to be healed"—future tense—you are not speaking in faith. Faith allows you to say "I *am* healed," regardless of what it looks like or feels like in the moment. And the same goes for getting a better job, paying the bills, finding the right wife or husband.

I'd never heard preaching like that in my whole life. The sermons I grew up hearing were highly emotional. *For the lord! Come here, let me smack you again. Hands up! Hallelujah! Hallelujah! Get the bucket out for the sixth time!* By the end, the preacher had 90 percent of your paycheck. I believed in the power of God, but somehow I never saw the results of his power. Why? Because I hadn't yet developed faith for it. *Real* faith.

Suburbs or not, I *needed* to go to Pastor Winston's church. The next Sunday morning, I drove out for one of the morning services.

The Living Word Christian Center had seating for ten thousand people, and the service was packed. Most of the people were African American, but all different races were represented. I'd never been to a church with different races before. Everyone was dressed in their Sunday best, all the men in suits. *Wow,* I thought, as I took a seat way in the back.

When Dr. Winston came out, I was not disappointed. In real life, he was even more challenging, inspiring, and thoughtful than the guy I'd listened to on the CDs. But then something happened that made me feel uncomfortable. Right in the middle of his sermon, Winston marched down the aisle and all the way back to my row. The scripture he was talking about happened to coincide with something I was going through personally, sex outside of marriage, so I was getting extra uneasy. I'd had enough "coincidences" that year to last me awhile, yet I was still clinging to the notion that was all it was—coincidence.

He then looked directly at me. Eye to eye. And his words got even more direct, more personal. He was almost verbatim using as a hypothetical example the exact circumstances of my life. He was, I thought, putting my business in the street. I felt convicted. I'd gone to churches where my grandmother would tell the pastor what was going on in my life, and he'd have some words for me during the service. That wasn't God talking; that was Nana. This was something else. Winston didn't know me from Adam, didn't even know I was coming, and had never met anyone in my family.

I was shaken. *If he looks at me again or gets too specific again, I'm out.* Pastor Winston returned to the front of the church, but later in the sermon, he came back and did the same thing—speaking about things I was going through. That was it. *I'm out of here!* As soon as he went back to the front, I left. I went home, embarrassed and determined never to return.

The next Sunday, I figured I'd tune in online to see what Winston was talking about. But that was all. My little brothers burst into the room and asked what I was watching. I told them I was "watching church." They just laughed.

The following week, I went back, despite my reservations. I attended Pastor Winston's 7 A.M., 9 A.M., *and* 11 A.M. services. I was *hungry* for God—the *active* God that people talked about at his church. There was something else, too: the power of seeing all these successful black people gathered in one place. Each person I met there had *this* business or *that* investment going on. It was inspiring.

My transformation had begun.

One of the very first things I did was buy some suits. Suits weren't required at my job, so I never wore one. But at this new church, all the men dressed like CEOs and politicians. So I went to a fashion superstore—a "buy one, get five free" kind of place—and splurged on a $100 suit. At church, I began sitting in the first or second row, right in there with Dr. Winston's own family.

The next thing I knew, I registered to attend a financial conference the church hosts every year. This wasn't some politician coming in to tell us how to vote. (In fact, when a politician visited *this* church, Winston never really let them speak at all. He'd just say, "We got Governor So-and-So here!") The only message or direction we were getting on Sunday was from scripture and the testimonies of one another's lives.

On the day of the conference, I was driving to the church in terrible traffic. "I'm gonna be so late," I said with a sigh. I decided to turn around and go back home. But then I heard a voice, as loudly as the night I'd been chased. *Just go! Just go!*

My instinct of *You're going to be late, just go home* had been an echo of the voices I'd heard throughout my life: "It's not going to work." "You can't do that." "You don't have the skills or schooling." "You don't have the money, the time" "That *never* works." "It's a one-in-a-million shot."

But the lessons from church had taught me to forget the naysayers. I now knew that God was going to talk me through *His* process.

Interestingly enough, I got to the conference *early*.

A crowd was already waiting to get in, an usher blocking the door. An older gentleman came walking in with a young man who appeared to be his son. Clearly the older man was somebody important at the church, because ushers were escorting him past the rest of us and through the main door.

"Just you and your son?" the usher asked. The man nodded.

"Can I be your son?" I stepped forward with a grin.

The guy smiled back, shook my hand, and invited me in. We

sat together at one of the big round conference tables, talking. He worked in real estate. "What did you do before?" I asked.

"Janitor," he said. Turns out he'd worked for a guy who'd suggested he invest in something. He invested in real estate and became a millionaire in his first year. From janitor to millionaire in the span of a single year. I am sure many would find that hard to believe. But, as Pastor Winston always told us, "you can be born across the tracks or even *on* the tracks, but that doesn't determine your outcome in life." I wanted to live that life myself.

By this time, the rest of the attendees had been let in, and people just kept walking up to our conversation. "I hear you talking real estate," one woman said. "I'm a realtor." Another woman said, "I've been listening to your conversation, and I am in the business as well. Can I join y'all?" I had a notepad out and wrote down everyone's information. A seed had been planted.

About a month or so later, God directed me back to that notepad, and I followed up with the two real estate ladies. One called back and we met, first talking faith and then business. At the time, I was working for the federal government and knew nothing about property or being a landlord. We filled out an application, and she ran my credit report to see what my options were.

I had zero credit rating. *Great!* I thought. *A clean slate!* But the woman politely explained that I *needed* a credit score to buy the property and told me we'd revisit the process again in a year. I thought, *A year is too long.* If God could make the whole universe in seven days, surely he could help me with my credit score.

I prayed and looked for guidance in the scriptures. "Father God, I thank and praise you . . . I receive a credit score above seven hundred." After a month, God told me to check my credit again.

I went and checked. Thirty days. *My God!*

I called my realtor. "My highest score is 735," I said.

"That's impossible," she replied. "There's no way something like that happened in thirty days."

"It's 735," I promised. "I'm seeing it right here."

"I don't even need to check because I know it didn't happen." She wouldn't budge. "Listen, send it to me in email. I'm not even gonna pull it because it costs *me* money."

I sent her a screen capture. Then she pulled it herself.

"What did you do?" she asked, marveling. "How is this possible?"

"I used the scripture," I said. "Colossians 2:14: 'Having canceled the charge of our legal indebtedness, which stood against us and condemned us; he has taken it away, nailing it to the cross.'"

"You used *what*?" This was a woman who was going to the same church I was. Her first question *should* have been: "What scripture did you use?"

In more practical terms, I had an unused credit card with a small limit, and I was led to use this credit card instead of my debit card and pay it off at the end of every week. Lo and behold, Citibank more than doubled my credit limit, and my credit score jumped up almost overnight. But the inspiration for *that* strategy *had* come from God.

So many people fail to capitulate to that small voice telling them to do X, Y, or Z. They discount themselves: *I can't do this because . . . I don't come from the right family. I don't have the right degree. This person may not like me. That person may not accept my call. I'll be embarrassed if it doesn't work out.* We don't want people to look at us as being different. We don't want to give others the opportunity to say something negative about us.

Even telling my experiences in this book could expose me to ridicule.

But more often than not, the people who find success are the ones willing to put themselves out there. Those willing to risk it all, to ask, to be embarrassed. What's a little embarrassment when you have God on your side?

AFTER ESTABLISHING that I finally had the credit and the money to get a mortgage, the realtor and I went on a search for apartment buildings. Some months after our first meeting, I purchased a multiunit apartment building. Months later, at age nineteen, I gave testimony in front of the whole ten-thousand-seat church about what had happened. It was a wonderful morning sharing about this miracle that had taken place in my life.

People want to go to church on Sunday to feel good. They feel good while they're there, but then when they leave, as Mark 4:15 says, "the enemy comes immediately to steal the seed sown." You feel good about the message for a couple hours . . . maybe. But does the time at church truly change you, day after day, week after week? Does it change the trajectory of your whole life?

It should.

I'm still learning. My faith is far from perfect.

And lessons often happen when you least expect them.

WHEN I WAS YOUNGER, I met a young lady who grabbed my attention in a major way. She was outstandingly beautiful, and we had many things in common. She came to church services with me and eventually decided to get baptized, rededicating herself to Christ. That was a powerful moment for me, and I felt truly blessed to be able to share this with her. When we first met, the guys she was dating had private jets and expensive cars. I couldn't compete with them financially, yet she kept calling me, wanting to spend time with me, to talk, to learn more about the church and God. Despite my not having the material wealth of the other men she'd dated, she told me she wanted to be my girlfriend.

In that exact moment, I heard the voice of God tell me, *Be a friend to her, help her, but do not get romantically involved with her.* The message was like the one I'd received on the day the gang chased me.

But this time, regrettably, I disobeyed.

"Trust in the Lord with all thine heart," Proverbs 3:5-6 says, "and lean not unto thine own understanding. In all thy ways acknowledge him, and he shall direct thy paths." The Bible also says that a warning comes before a fall.

We continued dating, but instead of our relationship growing deeper, things began to feel more and more unsettled. The woman I'd fallen in love with was receiving calls from other people late at night, and she would often disappear and couldn't be reached. Echoes of my childhood and my mother. I had no idea what was going on, and I got more and more concerned. When I questioned her about it, she always had a convenient answer. You may know where this is going . . . but I didn't.

One day, I'm ashamed to say, I got onto her smartphone— completely invading her privacy. I knew that I was firmly in the wrong. That I was being mistrustful, paranoid. But as I started reading her text messages, I started to cry. The first message I read was between her and her best friend. In it, she said, *I feel so bad about what I am doing to Gianno. The nicest and sweetest guy I've ever been with.*

And then everything became clear.

She'd been selling her time and body to men for extraordinary amounts of money. She no longer needed it, as she had other means of income, but she'd come to value it more than anything else in her life. Even me. This, I came to believe, was what God had been trying to save me from when I heard that voice say not to pursue her romantically. It was an experience that has haunted me for years and made me extremely distrustful of people. Not listening to God's voice is a mistake I've tried not to make since.

And today I can only imagine what God will do next in my life.

My path to a successful life began when I started studying scripture and listening to the voice that had been with me since the very beginning. It made me see past the limited vision I had of myself and of what was possible in my life. And even when I've messed up, there's been forgiveness and hope on the other side.

Too many of the churches I attended in my childhood created a victim mentality—a mentality, and a spirituality, in which God was seen as a savior who doesn't require anything from us. I've since learned that if we want *real* change in our lives, we can't just wait on God to swoop down and solve our problems.

The better way is partnering with God and taking personal responsibility. We need to listen for God's voice, trust it, and then act.

The communities most in need of direction have churches

and pastors who are able to share such a faith. The spiritual communities are already there. It's just a matter of switching the narrative.

Some years ago, Jack Abernethy, the former CEO of Fox News, invited me into his office for a career discussion. This was a big deal, because most of my colleagues hadn't yet had the honor of sitting down with the CEO. He asked me what my five-year plan was.

I sat back in my chair, wondering what he would think if I said what was truly in my mind and heart. That my conservatism and my work for Fox News was connected directly to my faith.

He waited for my answer.

Eventually, I spoke. "I don't have one," I said.

Now *he* sat back, looking confused. "Why?" he asked.

"What I believe is possible for me in five years," I said, "God can do in a month. With his guidance, I make goals, then meet them. And then exceed them."

Abernethy nodded. "Great response," he said.

I might not have said what I did, out of fear of being embarrassed if he saw things differently. But my faith spoke. And after years of making peace with it, I've learned to follow that voice.

9

SHARED WISDOM

MENTORSHIPS AND THE CAPACITY OF EXPERIENCE

A FEW YEARS AGO, my younger brother told us he wanted to be a WWE wrestler.

At the time, he was a sophomore in high school. He weighed 130 pounds fully dressed, and while it's true that he'd played a little football, I'd never known him to lift a dumbbell or do a push-up in his life. Everyone in the family laughed when he told us of his plan.

Everyone but me.

Because I know what it's like to have people laugh at your dreams. Dreams of becoming a landlord. Of working in D.C. Of running your own company. Of anything outside the norm of what everyone around you has achieved.

A few months later, I was in the Fox News greenroom, waiting to make an appearance on the *Kennedy* show, when another guest, Dolph Ziggler, came into the room. Dolph was two-hundred-plus pounds of muscle, with the kind of chiseled jaw you usually see only in comic books. A fifteen-year veteran of the WWE, he'd been crowned world champ several times.

I wasn't going to miss my chance to support my brother's aspirations. To cash in on some of my success for the sake of someone who was just getting started.

"I'm not familiar with the WWE," I said, shaking Dolph's hand, "but my little brother wants to be a professional wrestler."

He grinned as if he'd heard that a thousand times before. But I kept going.

"I'd love to get the three of us together for lunch sometime," I said. "I could fly him out to L.A., and we could meet. Just so he can talk to somebody who's actually in the business."

It was an attempt at being a mentor to my little brother. Providing encouragement. Providing contacts. Reaching out to a high-level person whom he would never have access to without a little help from someone further along the path than he is.

The lunch hasn't happened—yet. But, like the often untapped power of faith, the often untapped capacity of mentors is another force worth embracing. The experience and guidance of those who've gone before us is a means to personal growth and an upward mobility that can effect genuine change.

We don't need government handouts and solutions when the answer to our next move is often only one office or email or chance meeting away.

This is about more than mentoring kids from disadvantaged backgrounds or even supporting organizations that make such connections for kids. Both are fantastic starts. But, ultimately, simply handing someone a mentor is the same trap as handing someone a check for $1,000 and saying, "Go."

Without the foundation of understanding the true and full value of a mentor, and of the methods of developing mentors ourselves, we put our genuine personal and professional growth at risk.

WHILE WORKING as a consultant in D.C., I'd started appearing on national TV and writing for *The Washington Times* and *The Hill.*

When my name started appearing in the papers and online, I began to get a lot of outreach from younger people who wanted to meet with me. Just as *I* had done after first arriving in D.C., they were reaching out to get advice on how to survive, and thrive, in Washington politics. They'd write via LinkedIn or email and say: *Hey, I'd love to meet with you. I want to learn how you did X or how you did Y.* In other words, they were looking for a mentor.

Almost every one of them, I have to admit, was white.

They were good kids—ambitious, hoping to make a difference in the world—and they all seemed to understand the importance of mentors. Of course, this wasn't some innate understanding. It had been *taught* to them. Their parents, teachers, and peers had reinforced the fact that it was okay to ask for help. That there was no shame in reaching out to someone and risking the chance of being told, "No, I'm too busy," or never hearing back at all. They understood, from the experience of others, that was just part of the process.

This is not usually the case with people who come from marginalized environments. I wasn't taught to seek help when I was growing up. Rather, many in my neighborhood were too concerned about the possibility of being embarrassed to ask for help.

Teens and twentysomethings in the inner city are filled with self-doubt. They're already thinking, *If I reach out to this guy, he's not going to respond. Why even bother?* They are not willing to hear, "I can't meet with you," because they've been hearing that their whole life. The last thing they want to see is an email saying, "I don't have time for you." The last thing they need is *another* rejection.

To push past those rejections, you have to be appropriately . . . *aggressive.* That's one of the missing ingredients for a lot of folk who want to be successful.

Another barrier to reaching out to a possible mentor is being unwilling to open up to the notion that someone knows more than you. That it's not weak to admit when someone is higher up than you or ahead of you. In my neighborhood, admitting weakness of any kind was often, literally, a death sentence. We were trained from birth not to admit our shortcomings.

This was—and is—a unique double-edged sword: too insecure yet also too prideful to ask for help. Either can put you at a disadvantage when pursuing your dreams. For millions of people, the combination of the two is a ticket straight to nowhere.

WHEN I ENTER ANY NEW industry—from politics to consulting to TV news to show production to the book you're now reading— the first thing I do is seek out a mentor. I'm looking for two things.

1. Somebody who's powerful, is deeply established in the field, and has a track record of success that other people respect.

2. An individual who sees those same qualities in me. Somebody who truly believes *Man, Gianno, you're talented. You're*

smart. You've done some good things and can surely reach my level or even go beyond. Someone who can see the greatness in me.

My grandfather was my first mentor. You know this by now, because stories of his support are peppered throughout this book. He told me I could be anything, especially when I felt discouraged, when kids made fun of me, or when other family members said: *You're not going to be successful. You can't learn. You can't....* My grandfather was the one guy who reinforced the fact that I *was* smart, that I *could* make it, that I *could* do anything I wanted to professionally. Although he wanted me to run his plumbing business one day, he also supported the various notions I had about my own future.

When I was eighteen, working part-time for the Social Security Administration, my mentor was a man named Stephen Sullivan II. Stephen was an African American who'd risen to the level of executive officer, working right under the assistant regional commissioner. He was only twenty-seven but already had a hand in shaping policy for the entire agency.

I always made a point of dressing nicely for work, especially after buying suits for church. One day, Stephen commented on my suit, and I took it as a chance to express interest in connecting with him over lunch. We met in his office, and he talked frankly with me. He explained how things *really* worked at the agency. He even asked about my goals and career aspirations.

Over the next ten months, we'd meet for lunch as often as Stephen could. He taught me how to navigate a career in the Social Security Administration. He counseled me on everything from how to apply for jobs and which training courses to take to how to get to the highest levels of the agency. (He was later promoted to agency headquarters in Baltimore, and we stay in touch to this day.)

Some years later, when I moved to D.C., the entrepreneur and political commentator Armstrong Williams took on a similar role for me, giving me my first opportunity in media by offering me a job writing for *The Washington Times*. In short order, I was writing for a black conservative think tank called Project 21 and appearing on radio and cable news shows several months later.

ONE OF THE OTHER major mentors in my life is a woman only a few years older than me.

When I met her, I was living in D.C. and regularly appearing on CNN, but I had this burning desire to be on Fox News. It was the number one cable news network, leaned conservative, but still ran programs I found unbiased, fitting my own worldview and goals. So I really wanted to be in that space.

I got the email addresses of a couple of Fox News producers, but when I reached out to them, I didn't hear back. Clearly, I needed a break to help move things along.

On Twitter one day, someone posted a Fox News segment featuring an analyst named Eboni K. Williams. She was smart, a strong debater and communicator. The next time I guest-hosted Armstrong's radio show on SiriusXM, I contacted Eboni to invite her on as a guest. She agreed.

On the program that day, we ended up debating about Obama and some executive order on guns. It turned out she wasn't a by-the-book conservative, but more of an independent who leaned to the right. We went at it hard for twenty minutes, going back and forth. After the show, I gave her a call to say thanks and asked if she'd be open to talking with me sometime about television and her career. She texted me three days later and told me to let her know the next time I was in New York, and we could grab a beverage or coffee.

I was excited to sit down with someone who'd gone so far in her career. After all, Eboni had worked for CBS, HLN, and now Fox News. Surely she'd have some advice to share, as I had been coming up the media mountain for only a year. A few weeks later, I was in town and we met briefly right before she had an appearance on the *Megyn Kelly* show.

"Why did you want to meet with me?" Eboni asked toward the beginning of our conversation.

I replied simply, "You're young, black, and in media. So am I. I thought it would be great to connect. I'm always interested in hearing the stories of those in the media space. I'm still just learning the job."

She told me she'd been following my career. "Here's the good news," she said. "I want to help you."

I couldn't believe it. Here was this stranger saying that she believed in my goals and my ability to achieve them. That same night, as we were sharing our backstories and family histories, she told me her mom was a convicted felon. My heart leapt. Smart, successful, *and* she understood my plight.

"The next time you're in New York," she said, "let me know. I'll introduce you to some of the Fox News producers."

"I'll be back next Friday, then."

"*I'm* not going to be available next Friday," she said.

"Well, when *are* you available?"

"This Tuesday," she said. It was a Friday night.

"I'll see you then," I said. Just four days later, I bought the cheapest bus ticket I could find and made the four-hour trip from D.C. to New York. (You have to seize opportunities when they arise!)

Eboni met me at the front desk of the Fox building and signed me in. She took me down to the basement where all the Fox News producers worked, and introduced me to . . . everyone. "This is my friend," she said. "All you have to do is give him a topic and put a mic on, and he's ready to go."

At one point, Eboni asked a producer if she wanted to see my demo reel. "No," the producer replied. "Your word is good enough."

The very next week, they booked me on a show with Eboni live from New York.

Beyond making introductions, Eboni also offered advice. When the producers asked for my talking points—an idea of what I might say on topics X and Y—Eboni told me, "Don't give them the good stuff. Hold that for air. It makes it more authentic, and the producers will always be surprised and excited to hear you speak." That advice was perfect and has served me well through the years.

As I appeared on more shows over the next two months, Eboni watched every appearance, either live or on tape. She would call with advice. "Listen," she said one night. "Why is it that you go on looking so serious? What's this about? I know you used to get beat up on CNN, but this is Fox News. Come with the facts, but have fun at the same time."

Out of everybody in the media who's taken time to mentor me, Eboni has been my biggest advocate and teacher. Beyond being a peer mentor, she's also become a friend, a confidante, a sister. Someone I can truly share things with, whether it is about family, work, or situations nobody else would understand. I'm so thankful that a single tweet someone put online years ago changed the trajectory of my life.

IF I'M GOING TO mentor you, it's because I *know* you have the talent and potential to be successful. It's a powerful message— one that can change the course of another person's life.

This is precisely why we need to start more mentoring programs in our inner-city schools. The next generation needs to understand the benefits and virtues a mentor can offer and how to identify individuals who would make good mentors.

The primary reason many young whites are so willing to reach out for help is that most have seen mentoring done or have been told about it. They know, or have a good idea of, the steps involved, the possible rejection, and the advantages. Their neighbors had internships. Their friends have reached out to people who could tell them about a new trade or business opportunity. Their older brother told them how to follow up with someone after a first meeting.

Mentorship needs to be learned and modeled.

One group working to do just that is 100 Black Men of America. This worldwide organization began in 1963 in New York City when a small group of concerned African American men began meeting to explore ways of improving conditions in their community. The group included black businessmen, politicians, and industry leaders. Now with more than 10,000 members, these mentors are connecting with more than 100,000 minority youth annually. Their motto: "What They See Is What They'll Be." Local chapters, like the one in Chicago, are able to deliver unique mentoring initiatives tailored to the community.

When more schools, churches, and youth service organizations embrace similar opportunities and learning initiatives, more people in our inner cities will be able to grow with the wisdom of those who've come before us.

Part of being a conservative is believing that there's power in embracing the wisdom of what came before you. Of what has worked in the past. There are ideals and values and methods that are worth acquiring and carrying on. There are well-trodden paths that can lead to success and an openness to creating *new* paths and methodologies.

One of the first things we should teach in our schools is the art of reaching out for contacts. *Whom does your mentor know that you don't? To whom might they introduce you?* By asking these questions, you can quickly build a network of individuals who could prove quite helpful. If you want to be the best basketball player in the world, or the best entrepreneur, you'll want to talk to someone in that field. But even if you can't likely get hold of LeBron James or Bill Gates, somebody down the street probably has something to teach you about your area of interest. (Four years ago, I couldn't get Eboni to follow me on Twitter, but now we're good friends, and I'm having dinner and friendly conversations with folk like Ann Coulter and Bill Maher at the Polo Lounge in Beverly Hills.) Your list of contacts will grow every year when you stick your neck out, have the developing résumé to back it up, and get to know more and more people.

It helps that we live in the age of social media, which makes it far easier to reach out to people and start these discussions. Even now, there are people I reach out to—for instance, someone I've seen on television. I might direct message them on Twitter or email them and say, "Hey, I'd love to meet you and talk over coffee or dinner." Because I want to learn about them, but they're also interested enough to want to learn about me.

A good mentor can be someone you have never met face-to-face.

Dr. Winston, my spiritual adviser, and like a father to me for more than ten years now, became a mentor of mine without us ever having a conversation. I knew him through books and DVDs, online sermons. Today, however, Winston and I are close enough to meet for lunch or talk on the phone, but our mentor relationship existed long before he even knew who I was.

Among Winston's first mentors were the Tuskegee Airmen. He grew up in Tuskegee, Alabama, and was never far from these "larger-than-life heroes," as he called them. "These men greatly influenced my decision to become a pilot and enter the military after college. When I was growing up, most of the activities and life of Tuskegee were influenced by the military. We had black aviators like Chappie James living in our community. I had the privilege of knowing many of the legendary Tuskegee Airmen because their sons and daughters were my classmates in elementary school."

Those hoping to take the next steps just have to be ready, willing, and open to the wisdom of others who are further down a given path.

Someone may even read this book and decide *I'm* their mentor, even if we never meet in person.

ALL TOO OFTEN, people look at "mentor" as a mere title. As if being able to say "Oh, this is my mentor" is enough. As if having a mentor, as opposed to really tapping into the benefits of a mentor, is enough. Those new to being mentored need to learn to make regular contact with their mentor so they don't lose space in their mentor's head. Mentees need to get on the phone and ask for advice, for feedback, to make sure they're giving their mentor something to be proud of. Mentors should be able to see a mentee's hard work. If the mentee doesn't have something exciting to report every few weeks, they're simply not reaching their highest potential, not utilizing the opportunities and wisdom their mentor has provided.

There may come a time when you "outgrow" your mentor. Your career may surpass theirs, or you may move into another field altogether. Some mentors can even become a detriment. You might be in a place in your life where you need people around who are going to encourage you and be very positive, but your mentor, for any number of reasons, might no longer be able to provide that.

My grandfather was my first mentor, but there came a point when I progressed beyond his professional advice. He knew about owning and running a successful plumbing business, about customers, and about working with local government. He knew nothing about D.C. politics, consulting at the national level, or television. He remains my hero, but I must now look elsewhere for mentors in my professional life.

Another example is my father. Although I love my father and he has taught me a lot about many things, I can't count on him for true mentorship.

Recently, I told him I was planning to make a new business connection in L.A. He laughed, told me it'd never happen. I almost shouted in the middle of the restaurant: *Do you know who you're talking to? How many times I've been told, "No, it'll never happen"?*

That was exactly why I didn't tell him and many others in my family that I was buying an apartment building back in 2006. I didn't want the negativity. Whether it's becoming a landlord or a WWE wrestler, everyone who's pursuing a dream needs a mentor who may caution against folly but still believes in their ability to achieve their goal.

That's why it's so important to have people around you who recognize your potential and can enhance your productivity and help you get closer to your life goals. They won't shoot down your ideas or dreams. Instead, they'll think of ways to encourage them. They might give critical feedback, but they'll do it from a place of love and caring. They want to see you succeed.

Perhaps it's a little counterintuitive, but part of self-reliance is having the willingness and confidence to ask for and accept a little help. I reject the notion that the government is needed to give people a handout throughout their lives, but I know there are men and women out there ready to offer those following in their footsteps a hand up.

That's the conservative way.

THE TEST OF TIME

In early 2019, I was invited to Chicago to be the keynote speaker at an annual dinner for the DuPage County Republicans. DuPage County, you may recall, is where I started more than ten years ago, nervously walking into a room filled with older white men because I believed I was a conservative.

Many of those men were at this event. This time, the doughnuts had been replaced with chicken cordon bleu, and there were many other guests in attendance. Almost a thousand, including mayors, congressmen, and lieutenant governors. True to form for a big gathering of Republicans, there was also a guy dressed like Abraham Lincoln. Thankfully, though, no one brought hand-drawn signs or screamed once about Obama.

I gave my speech that night, a quick summary of the book you now hold in your hands. A story about where I came from and the values and people who've helped get me to where I am today. I spoke about freedom and faith and personal responsibility. And, while standing in new shoes from Paris with red bottoms, I spoke of the ones I'd once sold in D.C. for rent money.

Future plans I kept to myself that night, but I offered a call to action to everyone in the room—tables of college kids and retirees, politicians and Illinois kingmakers, even a billionaire real estate magnate (no, not Trump)—to seek excellence in their lives, to transform their conservative values into transformative action.

Seated next to the Illinois GOP power brokers were my little brother (the future WWE star), my cousin, my godmother, and old friends from years before. Some in the room were the same people who'd once predicted my early demise in Republican politics and in D.C. Now they were smiling, congratulating me, saying "Welcome home," just like those in the room who'd always had my back.

The night was one moment among many that continue to shape the man I am today. And it helps fuel my belief that we need to do a better job of communicating these conservative values to the people who need them the most.

In these pages, I've described the despondency and surrender that filled the tenement housing and neighborhoods where I grew up. It was a sickness passed down from generation to generation. An airborne contagion that infected every conversation, every government check, every conceding sigh. A disease that all too quickly overpowered my own grandmother.

I think back to that special report I did for Fox News, when I spoke with residents of the hardest-hit neighborhoods in my hometown. I spoke to grandmothers like my own, and to men who'd lost their businesses. I spoke with the gangbangers and drug dealers.

All had the same solution. They said that if real jobs were available, things would be better. The produce stores would return. The neighborhoods would be filled with children playing outside, ice cream trucks, people spending time together at night after a hard day's work. Even the gang members, many told me, would go legit. Meanwhile, they wait for someone else, the government, to provide those real jobs and opportunities.

But that isn't the answer. My grandfather's plumbing business struggled every day because of overregulation, high taxes, and our country's failed immigration policy. I'm a conservative because I know that the people of Chicago will have more jobs and places to work when government reduces regulations and taxes, puts aside liberal political posturing on the immigration challenge, and returns to the commonsense solutions Americans are screaming for.

An easy example: Liberals unwisely think that raising the minimum wage will make everything better for those who need higher-paying jobs. But what happens instead is that when companies are forced to overpay their employees, they hire fewer, cut hours, or let technology do the work people used to do. It's largely inner-city residents with the lowest job skills who suffer. In 1933, President Franklin Roosevelt signed the National Industrial Recovery Act and a minimum wage of $12 to $15 per week. The Supreme Court ruled the act unconstitutional in 1935, but the damage had already been done: Half a million black workers had lost their jobs.

For years, Americans of all political distinctions have bought the fallacy that Democrats "look out for the little guy." The blue-collar workers, the waitress, the janitor, the teacher, the local farmer, the union guy. The minorities. The poor.

However, the forgotten men and women of this country have

finally realized they've been taken for granted. Democrats have shown their hand—playing to the liberal elite and seeking votes from illegal immigrants, rather than supporting those, like union workers and the African American communities across the country, who've supported the Democrats for fifty-plus years.

The American people are finally fighting back. They realize that liberalism has failed them. It is a system that has both ignored them and created a foundation for failure; a system of dependency and surrender. A system of unaddressed violence. A system of controlling language so that only one voice, the liberal voice, can ever be heard.

I'm a conservative because I believe the free market would have better served those struggling Americans. While writing this conclusion, unemployment hit the lowest numbers in sixty years, and employment for minorities and women has never been higher. Trump, for all his imperfections, *did* deliver on the conservative promise of a country with fewer political decrees and wealth-redistributive taxes. America's businesses responded with a resounding *yes!*

I'm a conservative because I know that the people of Chicago—and St. Louis and Camden and New Orleans and Dayton—can reject unfulfilled liberal promises and return to their own core values. Values of self-dependency and strength. Values of real faith. Values that respect our language, our past, our laws.

And I'm a conservative for more personal reasons.

MY MOM, you'll be happy to hear, has been clean from drugs for more than a decade. Today, she lives in California and works as a nurse, caring for people whose journeys are similar to hers. She lives in a safer neighborhood and has a life that no longer drags her down with every breath.

The government did not do this for her. My local alderman did not do this. *She* did. Not with federal assistance or handouts, but because she was willing to do the hard work that was needed.

It started, she says, when she was re-baptized at a service I took her to at my church. My mother says she saw angels that day, and then everything changed. Maybe that sounds far-fetched to you. But if you've read this far into the book, you know where I stand on such things.

Whatever the catalyst, she went to various rehabs for years, calling on the same inner strength that kept her from ever missing a day at school. My mom got her own life back on track to become the woman she'd always wanted to be. Her struggle was long and hard—but she got through it.

During those years, she and I fought and reconciled and cried too many times to count. And through that process, we came to terms as mother and son. Some. Both of us know that there's still work to do. It's not always the easiest relationship to navigate, but it's one of the most important ones—the relationship that shapes a boy into a man and prepares him for all other emotional connections.

The painful memories from my childhood will never completely fade. I will never forget the time my mother slept outside my window and cried out loudly because my grandmother refused to let her in the house, or the time she tried physically fighting my grandmother (I forget why), or the many men she had sex with, men who were addicts themselves. I will always remember the secrets and lies. The disappearing acts. The addiction to short-term pleasure at long-term costs. Those memories bring me great anguish even to this day.

You may not have dealt with situations exactly like this, but I know I'm not alone in experiencing something that still hurts intensely, that dredges up feelings of pain and humiliation years after the fact. Maybe you've buried these situations inside in order to move forward in life, or maybe you deny that they ever happened. I've been there. I understand.

But as I've gotten older, I've come to understand several things. I've realized that despite the pain, I have core values I can always return to—values connected to faith and family, to discipline and hard work. I've prayed more and gone to church more. I've thrown myself more into work and my own career. I've returned to a stronger belief in self. I've realized that my desire to help others comes from a good place, a true place— *even if those I try to help don't always get better.* I've learned that human relationships can be full of disappointments and challenges, but that my personal relationship with God will sustain me in the face of anything. And that when He speaks in my heart, I should listen and trust in that still small voice that always speaks with righteous power.

I just hadn't realized it yet, but these are the lessons that served me long before my mother got better. And they are the lessons that have continued to serve me well ever since.

I'LL CLOSE BY SHARING one last story—this time from the realm of politics.

In my early twenties, I was working in downtown Chicago.

I'd already taken to wearing nicer clothing to work. It made me feel more capable and professional. Like I belonged. I had recently purchased a pair of Ferragamo shoes, which were the nicest footwear I'd ever owned. I wanted nothing more than to find a nice briefcase for work, and when I did, I purchased it. Never mind the $900 price tag. But I was proud of it, and it made me feel good.

Then I overheard some of my co-workers making fun of me, with my expensive shoes and my expensive briefcase. They could tell I was attempting to fit in, but they didn't want me to succeed in doing so. They didn't want me to dress too well or talk too loud or say too much.

I have a big personality. I know that. Long before I was on TV or commented on current events, I pushed myself into the conversation even when—*especially* when—I wasn't invited. It was clear that this particular group of people would rather have seen me stay in my place. The place for a young person, a guy from the South Side, a guy who was born across the tracks, who shouldn't dress in fancy clothes or take part in important conversations.

In that moment, I knew I had a choice. I could stay in my place, a place that had been assigned by those who knew nothing about me, or I could forge ahead, making my own way.

I chose to be me. With all my flaws, my rough edges, my fancy shoes, and my poverty-stricken past. I would honor the choices I made during times of great struggle and the choices I made because I was too blind to see the truth, and I would put forth my authentic self. I'd speak from a core place of my own personal power to whoever would listen, telling my stories and the stories of those around me with the passion and enthusiasm they deserved.

I would belong, because I *do* belong. Me and those fancy shoes that I ultimately ended up selling to make the rent in D.C.

I've shared a lot of personal stories in this book to demonstrate the experiences, some quite difficult, that have shaped my confidence and trust in my core values. We've all struggled in different ways and at different levels. Financially. Physically. Spiritually. And every one of us is going to be asked these questions: What do you stand for? What do you believe?

For some, the questions will be put to them as harshly as they were to me at all the turning points in my life. Seeing my mother in a period of great distress and asking, *What can I do?* Enduring the snide remarks of my co-workers who sought to keep me in my place, to not allow me to stand out, to keep my light dim and my voice lowered, and to not be the person I knew I could be.

And finally when I gave that keynote speech in Chicago, where I was challenged to take my message to the next level and step further along the path of breaking through perceived barriers, dismissing the status quo, explaining why I believe the things I do.

As an African American, as someone born into poverty and raised in an environment of hopelessness and crime, I believe that conservative ideals provide the best opportunity for a life beyond becoming a statistic. I would no longer be taken for granted. I have sought answers that have stood the test of time, embraced them, and put them to the test in my own life. I have taken my darkest moments and greatest obstacles as opportunities to identify what values are most important to me. Core values of family, faith, and self-worth.

I don't know what the next ten, twenty, or thirty years will bring for me, but I trust that the values that elevated and saved me will remain powerful and evident. I know that when we as a society follow these values, conservative values that reject dependence and embrace faith and self-determination, anything is possible. Anything at all.

Our future is of our own making.

And I know that it will be extraordinary.

ACKNOWLEDGMENTS

I wrote this book in answer to the two questions I'm most often asked: (1) How, considering your start, did you achieve what you have? (2) How/why the @%# are you a black conservative? If you've read the book, you'll see that the two answers are fundamentally intertwined. My sincerest hope in answering these two questions was to make, perhaps, some impact on the world by telling the stories of my life—some quite painful, some amusing, hopefully insightful and inspiring, and some very spiritual—to collectively put in motion for other people the ideals that have shaped my life. A spark, or *re*-spark, for those seeking something beyond their current life. That to be your greatest self, you *can* rely on these conservative values. Whatever your background, race, political party, and so on . . . they work.

This book has been a peculiar and illuminating journey—part memoir, part treatise on culture and politics—while exploring my own positions *and* digging back through my thoughts and experiences over the past almost thirty years. Thank you to those who helped me with this undertaking. Although this process took a year's worth of tears over painful memories, joy for the successes, and humility for the road still ahead, this acknowledgment section is perhaps the hardest thing I have had to write—for concern of leaving someone out. Knowing I didn't make it to this point alone, I want to thank the many who've helped me along the way:

To God, without whom this journey wouldn't be possible, and His voice which gives me instructions for the next level of life. To my pastor and spiritual father, Dr. Bill Winston, who made the time to discuss this book with me and whose teaching created a new reality in my life far bigger than anyone, including me, could have imagined. Thank you!

To my mother. Our journey has been filled with ups and downs, but God's love has seen us through. As I started the book, I told you that your life was the catalyst for my life's work and I would speak candidly about some of the difficult moments we've had. You understood. Thank you! I love and forgive you.

To family and friends who've answered questions and filled in the blanks, even when they understood some of the memories were not putting us all in the best light. Thank you and love you to my grandfather, my hero who always believed in me. To my grandmother, who selflessly took me and my siblings into her home many years ago. Your sacrifices were not in vain, and I hope I made you proud of the man I am today. To my dad, who was an active and caring father. To Aunt Patricia, who taught me what real and active faith is. My godmother, Barbara, who has supported my vision, my wildest dreams, my everything. My cousin Oluwatoyin, who's more like a sister, for keeping me sane and supporting me all these years. To Uncle Jamie, my little brother Matthew (the future WWE superstar), my other siblings, nephews, nieces, cousins, extended family, and the many who all have helped. Your life and support means so much to me.

To those friends and colleagues who provided much-needed feedback and encouragement: Eboni K. Williams, my dear friend and colleague in media—and also my sister not by blood, but certainly just as close. Thank you for believing in my talent many years ago. You took a chance and brought me into the largest media organization in the business and invested your time and resources in me, and I cannot thank you enough. All I can promise you is that I will continue to pass it on as you did for me many years ago; I love you, Sis.

To Neil Cavuto, thank you for believing in my talents and opening the door for me to join the Fox News family. There are so many who've invested in me and my career, please know I thank you all; there are drafts of this book which include dozens of more names.

To the publishing pros who've worked with me to make this book a reality, offering guidance and genuine care throughout: Derek Reed and the whole team at Crown Forum; the team at Foundry Literary + Media; Iris Bahr for getting things started; my agent Roger Freet who championed me throughout; special thanks to Geoffrey Girard, who shared in all the tears and laughter along the way and provided his skills, intelligence, and advice to help me make this the book I'd hoped for. I thank you, my friend.

To you, the reader, for joining me on this journey and being open to briefly share and explore another's path. I've learned a lot about myself during the more than year process of working on this book, and I sincerely hope you've gotten something out of my journey as well.

GIANNO CALDWELL is the founder of Caldwell Strategic Consulting, a bipartisan firm in Washington, D.C., that provides strategic advice and consulting in the areas of public affairs and government relations. For seventeen years, Gianno held various leadership roles at the federal, state, and local levels. He is a Fox News political analyst and correspondent for *The Hill,* providing commentary on political, financial, and cultural issues. He is also a special correspondent for *Extra,* covering red carpets in Hollywood and Washington, D.C.